STUDY GUIDE

Union with Christ

Sinclair B. Ferguson

I0808538

LIGONIER MINISTRIES
Renew your Mind.
LIGONIER.ORG | 800-435-4343

421 Ligonier Court, Sanford, FL 32771
Email: info@ligonier.org

Printed in China.

Contents

Introduction

What does it mean to be a Christian? Common answers to this question can be contradictory and confusing. Is Christianity simply an ethical system or a set of doctrinal beliefs? In *Union with Christ*, Dr. Sinclair Ferguson surveys one of the Apostle Paul's favorite phrases to describe the essence of the Christian life: being "in Christ." This twelve-part teaching series explores what it means to be "in Christ" and how these two simple words can reshape our entire existence.

This study guide is a companion to the video teaching series. Whether you are using the DVDs, streaming the videos on Ligonier.org, or going through the course in Ligonier Connect, this resource is designed to help you make the most of the learning experience. For each message in the series, there is a corresponding lesson in this guide. Here is what you will find in each lesson:

INTRODUCTION	The introduction is a brief paragraph that summarizes the content covered in the lecture and considered in the study guide lesson. **How to use:** Use the introduction to each lesson to get a sense of the big picture before watching the video. Refer to these statements as you work through the study guide to remind yourself of what you have already covered and where you are headed.
LEARNING GOALS	The learning goals are the knowledge and skills the study guide lesson will endeavor to equip you with as you work through the lecture content. **How to use:** Familiarize yourself with the goals of each lesson before engaging with its contents. Keeping the overall purpose in mind as you watch each video and reflect on or discuss the questions will help you get the most out of each lesson.
KEY IDEAS	The key ideas are the major points or takeaways from the lecture. **How to use:** Use these ideas to prepare yourself for each lesson and to review previous lessons. They describe specifically the knowledge each lecture is communicating.

REFLECTION & DISCUSSION QUESTIONS	The questions are the guided reflection and/or discussion component of the lesson that are intended to help you prepare for, process, and organize what you are learning. **How to use:** Reflect on individually or discuss in a group the questions in the order in which they appear in the lesson. The time stamps in the right margin indicate where the answers to questions during the video can be found.
PRAYER	The prayer section offers suggestions for how to close the lesson in prayer with respect to what was taught in the lecture. **How to use:** Consider using each lesson's prayer section as a guide to personal or group prayer. These sections follow the ACTS prayer model, which you can learn more about in R.C. Sproul's Crucial Questions booklet *Does Prayer Change Things?* This helpful guide is available as a free e-book at Ligonier.org.
REVIEW QUIZ	The review quiz is a set of six multiple-choice questions that appears at the end of each lesson. **How to use:** Use each quiz to check your comprehension and memory of the major points covered in each lecture. It will be most beneficial to your learning if you take a lesson's quiz either sometime between lessons or just before you begin the next lesson in the study guide.
ANSWER KEY	The answer key provides explanations for the reflection and discussion questions and answers to the multiple-choice questions in the review quiz. **How to use:** Use the answer key to check your own answers or when you do not know the answer. Note: Do not give in too quickly; struggling for a few moments to recall an answer reinforces it in your mind.

Study Schedules

The following table suggests four plans for working through the *Union with Christ* video teaching series and this companion study guide. Whether you are going through this series on your own or with a group, these schedules should help you plan your study path.

	Extended 14-Week Plan	**Standard 12-Week Plan**	**Abbreviated 6-Week Plan**	**Intensive 4-Week Plan**
Week	**Lesson**			
1	*	1	1 & 2	1–3
2	1	2	3 & 4	4–6
3	2	3	5 & 6	7–9
4	3	4	7 & 8	10–12
5	4	5	9 & 10	
6	5	6	11 & 12	
7	6	7		
8	7	8		
9	8	9		
10	9	10		
11	10	11		
12	11	12		
13	12			
14	*			

* For these weeks, rather than completing lessons, spend your time discussing and praying about your learning goals for the study (the first week) and the most valuable takeaways from the study (the last week).

1

"In Christ"

INTRODUCTION

Some of the ways in which evangelicals self-identify today were not part of the vernacular of early believers. The first Christians thought of themselves as followers of "the Way" and as being "in Christ." In this lesson, Dr. Ferguson reasserts this ancient way of thinking about the Christian life, and he demonstrates how the doctrine of union with Christ, which is often overlooked today, actually resides at the heart of Christian faith and life.

LEARNING GOALS

When you have finished this lesson, you should be able to:

- Describe why the idea of being "in Christ" is important
- Summarize some effects of being united to Christ described in the book of Ephesians

KEY IDEAS

- The expression "in Christ" is an overlooked yet crucial way in which Scripture describes the Christian life.
- By being united to Jesus Christ, believers become citizens of a new kingdom.
- It is through union with Christ that believers experience the riches of the gospel.

REFLECTION & DISCUSSION QUESTIONS

Before the Video

What Do You Think?

Take a moment to answer the following questions. They will prepare you for the lecture.

- What words do you use most frequently to describe your religious affiliation? Why do you gravitate toward those particular words?

- When you think about the idea of union with Christ, what comes to your mind? What would you like to learn in this teaching series on the subject?

Scripture Reading

Blessed be the God and Father of our Lord Jesus Christ, who has blessed us in Christ with every spiritual blessing in the heavenly places, even as he chose us in him before the foundation of the world, that we should be holy and blameless before him. In love he predestined us for adoption to himself as sons through Jesus Christ, according to the purpose of his will, to the praise of his glorious grace, with which he has blessed us in the Beloved. In him we have redemption through his blood, the forgiveness of our trespasses, according to the riches of his grace, which he lavished upon us, in all wisdom and insight making known to us the mystery of his will, according to his purpose, which he set forth in Christ as a plan for the fullness of time, to unite all things in him, things in heaven and things on earth. In him we have obtained an inheritance, having been predestined according to the purpose of him who works all things according to the counsel of his will, so that we who were the first to hope in Christ might be to the praise of his glory. In him you also, when you heard the word of truth, the gospel of your salvation, and believed in him, were sealed with the promised Holy Spirit, who is the guarantee of our inheritance until we acquire possession of it, to the praise of his glory.

—Ephesians 1:3–14

- What are the spiritual realities "in Christ" that Paul presents in this passage?

During the Video

Answer the following questions while you watch the video. They will guide you through the lecture.

Little Preposition, Great Noun — *0:00–14:13*

- How many times does the word *Christian* appear in the New Testament? In what contexts does this word appear?

- How does Paul suggest that Christians are citizens of two different worlds in Ephesians 1?

Effects of Being in Christ *14:13–22:59*

- What are some of the benefits and implications of a believer's union with Christ that Paul describes in Ephesians 2–6?

- Why can life often seem to become more difficult after someone becomes a Christian?

After the Video

Answer the following questions after you have finished the lecture. They will help you identify and summarize the major points.

- What connotation did the term *Christian* originally carry? What are some examples of this kind of usage today?

  If you are in a group, have the members discuss how Christians are perceived in our culture today. In what ways do you think Christians are most commonly misunderstood?

- The reality of spiritual warfare can make life seem harder for a Christian than a non-Christian. In this warfare, what is Satan able to accomplish and not able to accomplish against Christians?

  If you are in a group, have the members read Ephesians 6:10–20. What great assurances can be drawn from this passage for our encouragement?

- What language does the New Testament use to describe a person's coming to faith in Christ? How does this language compare to the language that dominates today's evangelical subculture?

  If you are in a group, have the members discuss which of these descriptions they consider most accurate and why. What other descriptions of our new life in Christ have you found helpful?

PRAYER

Commit what you have learned from God's Word in this lesson to prayer.

- Praise God for two or three specific blessings that are yours in Christ.
- Confess ways that you have underappreciated your relationship with Jesus or taken it for granted.

- Thank God for giving you a new spiritual life and a new identity in Jesus Christ.
- Ask God to help you grow in both knowledge and praise during this study.

REVIEW QUIZ

Use these multiple-choice questions to measure what you learned from this lesson.

1. The word *Christian* most likely originated as a pejorative term.
   a. True
   b. False
2. Which of the following phrases did members of the early church use most frequently to describe themselves?
   a. Apostles
   b. Believers
   c. Christians
   d. Followers of the Way
3. According to Dr. Ferguson, who is the "man in Christ" mentioned in 2 Corinthians 12:2?
   a. Barnabas
   b. Paul
   c. Peter
   d. Timothy
4. How many times does Paul use language such as "in Christ" to describe Christians?
   a. 5 or fewer
   b. 25
   c. 63
   d. 80 or more
5. The statement "Ephesians 1 should never be read in church; it should always be sung" is attributed to which of the following theologians?
   a. B.B. Warfield
   b. John Calvin
   c. Jonathan Edwards
   d. Robert Murray M'Cheyne
6. Which of the following is in the power of Satan and his minions to accomplish?
   a. Defeating the church
   b. Destroying the salvation of believers
   c. Eroding a Christian's assurance of salvation and enjoyment of salvation
   d. Ruining God's purpose for a Christian's life

Answer Key—"In Christ"

REFLECTION & DISCUSSION QUESTIONS

Before the Video

What Do You Think?

These are personal questions. The answers should be based on your own knowledge and experience.

Scripture Reading

- What are the spiritual realities "in Christ" that Paul presents in this passage?

  Ephesians 1:3–14 offers a detailed summary of the benefits that believers share "in Christ." According to this passage, it is in Him that believers experience every spiritual blessing. In Christ, believers were chosen before the foundation of the world, and they have been redeemed through His blood. God's purpose to unite all things in Christ has been set forth in Him and enacted in the fullness of time. In Christ, believers have placed their hope and have obtained their inheritance. Moreover, in Christ, believers have been sealed with the Holy Spirit as a guarantee of that eternal inheritance. From beginning to end, it is in Christ that believers experience all the benefits of redemption both in this life and in the life of the world to come.

During the Video

Little Preposition, Great Noun

- How many times does the word *Christian* appear in the New Testament? In what contexts does this word appear?

  The word Christian *appears only three times in the New Testament. The first appearance is in Acts 11:26, which notes that followers of Jesus were first called Christians in the city of Antioch. The term appears again several chapters later in Acts 26:28, when Agrippa asks Paul if he thought he could persuade him so quickly to become a Christian. The third appearance of this term is in 1 Peter 4:16, when Peter deals with the topic of suffering as a Christian.*

- How does Paul suggest that Christians are citizens of two different worlds in Ephesians 1?

  In the opening verse of his letter to the Ephesians, Paul refers to the dual citizenship of Christians. He addresses this epistle "to the saints who are in Ephesus, and are faithful in Christ Jesus" (1:1). The first half of this description recognizes the physical, earthly location and citizenship of his readers. The second half reveals the spiritual allegiance that unites all believers, regardless of their physical surroundings. Consequently, Christians who dwell in different earthly cities belong to the same heavenly city. All who are in Christ serve the same King.

Effects of Being in Christ

- What are some of the benefits and implications of a believer's union with Christ that Paul describes in Ephesians 2–6?

  In Ephesians 2, Paul celebrates the reality that believers who were once dead in trespasses are now raised up to new life in Christ. Ephesians 3 discusses the wonder of having one's eyes opened to the eternal purposes of God that have been made known in the church, the assembly of those who are in Christ. In Ephesians 4, Paul elaborates on the union with one another that occurs as a result of being united with Christ. In Ephesians 5, he examines the clash of worlds that takes place as the implications of being in Christ are applied to Christians' relationships with their family members and others around them. Finally, Ephesians 6 concludes with instructions on how to engage in the spiritual warfare that results from one's new identity in Christ.

- Why can life often seem to become more difficult after someone becomes a Christian?

  Dr. Ferguson noted that many Christians find life to be laden with new difficulties after they receive Christ as Savior. This is true because the powers of darkness that once reigned over believers when they were dead in their sins now actively wage war against them. Those who follow Christ will find that all the power of hell is let loose against them because of their allegiance to Him.

After the Video

- What connotation did the term *Christian* originally carry? What are some examples of this kind of usage today?

  Christian *was originally a pejorative term that people in the first century used to express their disdain for the early church. Dr. Ferguson cited the contemporary word* fundamentalist *as an example of how descriptions of certain groups of Christians today are sometimes derogatory. Additional examples may come to mind based on your own experience.*

- The reality of spiritual warfare can make life seem harder for a Christian than a non-Christian. In this warfare, what is Satan able to accomplish and not able to accomplish against Christians?

  Satan and his minions are now unable to attack Jesus directly, so they actively wage war against His followers. No matter how fierce their spiritual onslaughts may be, they are unable to destroy the salvation of believers. Nevertheless, they will attempt everything in their power to undermine a Christian's assurance of salvation and enjoyment of that salvation in this life.

- What language does the New Testament use to describe a person's coming to faith in Christ? How does this language compare to the language that dominates today's evangelical subculture?

  References in the New Testament to Christ's "coming in" to a person's life are limited. The New Testament primarily uses language about sinners' needing to get out of themselves and get into the riches of Christ. Rather than conceiving of Christ as entering into sinners, Scripture describes conversion as sinners' entering into Christ. On the other hand, today's evangelical subculture relies heavily on language of Jesus' entering the lives of sinners. Many Christians can recall being encouraged at the time of their conversion to "let Jesus in," a notion that does not explicitly appear in Scripture.

REVIEW QUIZ

Lesson 1

1. **A.**
   The term Christian *first appears not on the lips of believers to describe themselves, but on the lips of nonbelievers to describe followers of Jesus (Acts 11:26; 26:28). In all likelihood, this was a pejorative term used to express disdain for the early church.*

2. **D.**
   The primary phrase used by Christians to describe their faith throughout the book of Acts is "the Way." This term appears as the early name for the Christian faith in Acts 9:2; 16:17; 18:25–26; 19:9; 19:23; 22:4; 24:14; and 24:22.

3. **B.**
   Dr. Ferguson argues that the "man in Christ" mentioned in 2 Corinthians 12:2–4 who "was caught up into paradise . . . and . . . heard things that cannot be told, which man may not utter" is actually Paul himself. Paul's detailed description of this event suggests that he was intimately familiar with this man's experience. By attributing it to "a man in Christ," Paul is able to describe this event in order to make a point to his readers without coming across as boasting about what he had experienced.

4. **D.**
   Based on the number of uses, language such as "in Christ" appears to be Paul's preferred way of talking about followers of Jesus. In his letters, he often speaks of himself as being "in the Lord," "in Him," or "in the Lord Jesus Christ." In all, he employs such phrases more than eighty times.

5. **A.**
The great Princeton theologian B.B. Warfield once remarked that Ephesians 1 should never be read in church but should instead be sung. This statement highlights the abundant joy that the message of this chapter can produce in the hearts of believers as they begin to fathom the incredible riches that are theirs in Christ Jesus.

6. **C.**
While Satan and his minions can never defeat Christ or His church, destroy a believer's salvation, or ruin God's plans for a Christian's life, the forces of darkness can and often do destroy a Christian's assurance of salvation and enjoyment of salvation.

2

Getting into Christ

INTRODUCTION

One of the great mysteries of redemption is the Holy Spirit's process of transforming enemies of Christ into coheirs with Christ. Few stories in Scripture illustrate this mystery as vividly as the conversion of the Apostle Paul. In this lesson, Dr. Ferguson recounts Paul's conversion by way of Philippians 3 to show how everything in Paul's life changed when he got out of himself and got into Christ Jesus.

LEARNING GOALS

When you have finished this lesson, you should be able to:

- Describe the Apostle Paul's process of coming to faith in Christ
- Identify factors that influence a believer to seek and savor union with Jesus

KEY IDEAS

- Rich in human accomplishments as a Pharisee, Paul was unaware of his need for Christ.
- Paul violently persecuted the church, but in the moment he came to faith in Christ, he profoundly understood the reality of union with Christ.
- The more Paul grew to know Christ, the more deeply still he longed to know Christ.

REFLECTION & DISCUSSION QUESTIONS

Before the Video

What Do You Think?

Take a moment to answer the following questions. They will prepare you for the lecture.

- How have your accomplishments shaped your identity?

- How did you become aware of your need for Christ?

Scripture Reading

What then shall we say? That the law is sin? By no means! Yet if it had not been for the law, I would not have known sin. For I would not have known what it is to covet if the law had not said, "You shall not covet." But sin, seizing an opportunity through the commandment, produced in me all kinds of covetousness. For apart from the law, sin lies dead. I was once alive apart from the law, but when the commandment came, sin came alive and I died. The very commandment that promised life proved to be death to me. For sin, seizing an opportunity through the commandment, deceived me and through it killed me. So the law is holy, and the commandment is holy and righteous and good.

—Romans 7:7–12

- How does Paul describe the law in this passage? How did the law bring Paul to an awareness of his own sinfulness?

During the Video

Answer the following questions while you watch the video. They will guide you through the lecture.

Paul's Life outside Christ *0:00–11:02*

- Who are the "dogs" that Paul mentions in Philippians 3:2?

- Before his conversion, how did Paul's attitude toward the early church differ from that of his mentor Gamaliel?

Paul's Journey into Christ *11:02–23:30*

- What are the two options people have when they encounter the Lord Jesus Christ in the life of a believer? How did Paul initially respond to the presence of Christ in Stephen's life?

- Describe the "holy dissatisfaction" that Paul mentions in Philippians 3.

After the Video

Answer the following questions after you have finished the lecture. They will help you identify and summarize the major points.

- Read Philippians 3:4–6. What moral credentials did Paul possess before he knew Christ?

  If you are in a group, have the members identify and share some of the ways they thought about themselves and were inclined to boast before they knew Christ.
- What does Dr. Ferguson mean when he says that Paul once had no real "sin consciousness"? What does it mean to be conscious of one's sins?

  If you are in a group, have the members describe their own process of becoming conscious of their sins. What do they do with their guilt?
- How do the life and death of Stephen illustrate principles that Paul presents in Philippians 3?

  If you are in a group, have the members identify and describe people they have known who, like Stephen, have been "full of grace." What was it like to be around them? How did they interact with others?

PRAYER

Commit what you have learned from God's Word in this lesson to prayer.

- Praise God for His sovereign role in leading sinners to repentance and faith in Christ.
- Confess areas of your life where you are tempted to boast apart from Christ.
- Thank God for providing a Savior for you and convicting you of your need for a Savior.
- Ask God to help you know Christ more fully and share in His suffering, death, and resurrection.

REVIEW QUIZ

Use these multiple-choice questions to measure what you learned from this lesson.

1. How many times does the account of Paul's conversion appear in the book of Acts?
   a. One
   b. Two
   c. Three
   d. Four

2. Which leader of the Pharisees advocated a policy of tolerance toward the early church?
   a. Caiaphas
   b. Gamaliel
   c. Nicodemus
   d. Saul
3. Which of the Ten Commandments led Paul to an awareness of his need for a Savior?
   a. "Remember the Sabbath day, to keep it holy."
   b. "Honor your father and your mother."
   c. "You shall not murder."
   d. "You shall not covet."
4. Paul belonged to which of the following Jewish groups represented by the synagogue mentioned in Acts 6:9?
   a. Alexandrians
   b. Freedmen
   c. Cilicians
   d. Cyrenians
5. Stephen is the only follower of Jesus in the New Testament to refer to Jesus as which of the following?
   a. Christ
   b. King of kings
   c. The Son of Man
   d. The True Vine
6. According to Paul, what is the "one thing" to which his life was devoted?
   a. Composing pastoral letters to the church
   b. Establishing new churches
   c. Proclaiming God's Word
   d. Pursuing the knowledge of Christ

Answer Key—Getting into Christ

REFLECTION & DISCUSSION QUESTIONS

Before the Video

What Do You Think?

These are personal questions. The answers should be based on your own knowledge and experience.

Scripture Reading

- How does Paul describe the law in this passage? How did the law bring Paul to an awareness of his own sinfulness?

  In these verses, Paul affirms that the law is not sinful but rather is holy, righteous, and good. One of the effects of the law in Paul's life was that it led to an awareness of his own sin. His sinful nature led him to violate the law's command not to covet. If the command not to covet had never been given, Paul would have remained unaware of his sin.

During the Video

Paul's Life outside Christ

- Who are the "dogs" that Paul mentions in Philippians 3:2?

  The "dogs" mentioned by Paul in Philippians 3:2 are a group known as the Judaizers. They taught that true Christians must not only believe in Jesus but also receive the sign of circumcision and follow Jewish regulations. Paul vehemently resisted this false teaching that people need something in addition to Christ to be saved. He consistently affirmed that in Christ alone believers possess everything that is needed to please God.

- Before his conversion, how did Paul's attitude toward the early church differ from that of his mentor Gamaliel?

  The Pharisee Gamaliel's attitude toward the early church appears in Acts 5:34–39. He urged the Jewish leaders not to resist the early believers. Instead, he contended that if Christianity was false, it would fade away on its own, and if Christianity was true, then it would be useless to resist it. In contrast to Gamaliel's tolerant mind-set, his student Paul violently persecuted the church in an effort to destroy it.

Paul's Journey into Christ

- What are the two options people have when they encounter the Lord Jesus Christ in the life of a believer? How did Paul initially respond to the presence of Christ in Stephen's life?

  Dr. Ferguson points out that when people encounter the Lord Jesus Christ in the life of a believer, they have only two options. The first option is to attempt to defy Him. The second option is to yield to Him and enter into a relationship with Him. Paul's initial response to the life of Christ manifested in Stephen was to seek Stephen's death and attempt to eradicate as many other Christians as possible.

- Describe the "holy dissatisfaction" that Paul mentions in Philippians 3.

  In Philippians 3, Paul expresses a profound sense of holy dissatisfaction. On the one hand, he is absolutely satisfied in Christ. On the other hand, he is not satisfied with how much he knows of Christ. As a result, he is relentlessly driven to pursue greater intimacy with his risen Lord.

After the Video

- Read Philippians 3:4–6. What moral credentials did Paul possess before he knew Christ?

  Compared to his peers, Paul possessed the highest possible credentials for a Jew of his day. He was a circumcised Jew of the tribe of Benjamin, a Hebrew of Hebrews who adhered flawlessly to the rigorous moral code of the Pharisees. He was morally blameless by the standards of the Jewish law and was zealous in his efforts to persecute those whom he perceived to be a threat to the Jewish faith.

- What does Dr. Ferguson mean when he says that Paul once had no real "sin consciousness"? What does it mean to be conscious of one's sins?

  As Dr. Ferguson explained, it is possible for people to be cognitively aware that they are not morally perfect without having a specific moral conviction of their own sins. Most people have no real sin consciousness and therefore consider themselves basically good. Without an awareness of their sin problem, people will never seek a Savior. This was the state Paul was in before the weight of his sinfulness had impressed itself on him.

- How do the life and death of Stephen illustrate principles that Paul presents in Philippians 3?

  In Philippians 3:10, Paul expresses his longing to share in Christ's sufferings and become like Him in His death and resurrection. Years earlier, Paul had witnessed this similarity to Christ in the martyrdom of Stephen. Stephen was full of grace. As he died, Stephen prayed a prayer similar to the one Jesus prayed on the cross. In his final moments, Stephen beheld the Son of Man standing at the Father's right hand. Like Jesus, Stephen was like a seed planted in the ground that bore abundant fruit in the lives of others.

REVIEW QUIZ

Lesson 2

1. **C.**
   The story of Paul's conversion is narrated three times in Acts. Luke first records Paul's conversion in Acts 9, and Paul proceeds to share his testimony with others in Acts 22:3–21 and 26:9–18.

2. **B.**
   Acts 5:34–39 records that on one occasion when Christians were on trial before the Jewish council, Gamaliel, a leader of the Pharisees and a teacher of Paul, argued that the Jewish authorities should take no action against the Christians. He argued that if Christianity was of human origins, it would fade away on its own, and that if it was of divine origins, resisting it would be futile.

3. **D.**
   Writing in Romans 7:7–9, Paul confides that his sinful nature led him to violate the command not to covet. In this way, the law revealed his sinful moral condition and his need for a Savior.

4. **C.**
   Stephen, the first Christian martyr, faced opposition from the synagogue "of the Freedmen and . . . , of the Cyrenians, and of the Alexandrians, and of those from Cilicia and Asia" (Acts 6:9). Paul, who was born in Tarsus in the region of Cilicia, would have belonged to this synagogue, and it is probable that he was one of the individuals who engaged in debate with Stephen before Stephen's trial and execution.

5. **C.**
   Jesus referred to Himself most frequently as the Son of Man. It is therefore noteworthy that Stephen is the only Christian in the New Testament who refers to Jesus in the same way (Acts 7:56).

6. **D.**
   Even though Paul accomplished a myriad of things for Christ during his ministry, in his mind everything that he did fit into the category of pursuing greater knowledge of Christ (Phil. 3:8, 13–14).

3

Dimensions of Our Union

INTRODUCTION

What is the defining reality of the Christian life? Is it freedom from sin? Is it living by faith? Is it the hope of heaven? As Dr. Ferguson reminds us, the defining reality of the Christian life is knowing Jesus and being united to Him. In this lesson, we will turn our attention to the centrality of Jesus Christ as the source of all other spiritual blessings and examine three foundational dimensions of a believer's union with the Lord Jesus.

LEARNING GOALS

When you have finished this lesson, you should be able to:

- Articulate why a focus on the person of Jesus Christ is vital to the Christian life
- Identify and describe three realities on which a believer's union with Christ is grounded

KEY IDEAS

- The greatest blessing of being united to Jesus is intimacy with Jesus.
- A believer's union with Christ is experienced through faith but grounded in God's eternal purpose, Jesus' incarnation, and our bonding of ourselves to Him in faith.
- The redemptive work of Jesus is of no practical value apart from the person of Jesus.

REFLECTION & DISCUSSION QUESTIONS

Before the Video

What Do You Think?

Take a moment to answer the following questions. They will prepare you for the lecture.

- What steps are involved in becoming a Christian? At what point does a person become united to Jesus Christ?

- If you are married, what do you love most about your spouse? If you are not married, what aspect of a married couple's affection for each other seems most important? Why?

Scripture Reading

> *Therefore, if anyone is in Christ, he is a new creation. The old has passed away; behold, the new has come. All this is from God, who through Christ reconciled us to himself and gave us the ministry of reconciliation; that is, in Christ God was reconciling the world to himself, not counting their trespasses against them, and entrusting to us the message of reconciliation. Therefore, we are ambassadors for Christ, God making his appeal through us. We implore you on behalf of Christ, be reconciled to God. For our sake he made him to be sin who knew no sin, so that in him we might become the righteousness of God.*
>
> —2 Corinthians 5:17–21

- What does this passage teach about being "in Christ"?

During the Video

Answer the following questions while you watch the video. They will guide you through the lecture.

No Blessings without the Person *0:00–7:50*

- Why is the concept of the golden chain helpful? What is missing from this concept?

- How does 1 Corinthians 6:15–20 reveal the power of a believer's union with Christ?

Three Dimensions of Our Union *7:50–23:05*

- What are the three major aspects of union with Christ?

- What do we know of Jesus' life between the ages of twelve and thirty? How does this knowledge enhance our understanding of His relationship with the Father?

- What kind of vocabulary does Paul use to describe belief in Christ? How does this compare to other ancient Greek writings?

After the Video

Answer the following questions after you have finished the lecture. They will help you identify and summarize the major points.

- How might Christians be in danger of focusing on the spiritual blessings that Christ offers without focusing on Christ Himself?

  If you are in a group, have the members identify and discuss ways to maintain a central focus on the person of Christ instead of merely focusing on His benefits.
- What does it mean that a believer's union with Christ is experienced through faith but is not grounded in faith? How can this truth encourage Christians who falter?

  If you are in a group, have the members describe a time when their faith has faltered or been challenged. What sustained their faith during that time?
- How does the reality of living in a different country from one's birth illustrate Paul's point in 2 Corinthians 5:17?

  If you are in a group, have the members describe some cross-cultural experiences that they have had. How can experiencing a different culture deepen one's understanding of what it means to live as citizens of two different worlds?

PRAYER

Commit what you have learned from God's Word in this lesson to prayer.

- Praise God for His eternal decree that has brought about your union with Jesus.
- Confess ways that you have cherished the blessings of Christ apart from Christ Himself.
- Thank God for sending an incarnate Savior who can identify with your human struggles.
- Ask God to help you experience greater joy and intimacy with Jesus.

REVIEW QUIZ

Use these multiple-choice questions to measure what you learned from this lesson.

1. Which of the following is *not* a dimension of union with Christ explored in this lesson?
    a. It is grounded in a believer's act of bonding to Christ in faith.
    b. It is grounded in Christ's incarnation.
    c. It is grounded in God's eternal election.
    d. It is grounded in the good works that a believer performs.
2. Faltering in faith does not cause a believer to falter in union with Christ.
    a. True
    b. False
3. Which grammatical phrase best describes Paul's understanding of faith?
    a. Believing "about Christ"
    b. Believing "in Christ"
    c. Believing "into Christ"
    d. Believing "on Christ"
4. The spiritual reality of union with Christ is patterned after the God-ordained institution of marriage.
    a. True
    b. False
5. According to Dr. Ferguson, which of the following is the most accurate translation of 2 Corinthians 5:17?
    a. "If any in Christ, new creation."
    b. "If any man be in Christ, he is a new creature."
    c. "If anyone is in Christ, he is a new creation."
    d. "If anyone is in Christ, the new creation has come."
6. Which of the following theologians wrote that all Christ has done remains "useless" to us "as long as Christ remains outside of us and we are separated from Him"?
    a. B.B. Warfield
    b. John Calvin
    c. Jonathan Edwards
    d. Martin Luther

Answer Key—Dimensions of Our Union

REFLECTION & DISCUSSION QUESTIONS

Before the Video

What Do You Think?

These are personal questions. The answers should be based on your own knowledge and experience.

Scripture Reading

- What does this passage teach about being "in Christ"?

  Paul proclaims that all who are found in Christ are a new creation; their former sinful selves have passed away, and they have become participants in a new creation. This is true because God has reconciled the world to Himself in Christ, and in Christ those who believe have become Christ's righteousness. Therefore, those who are in Christ are both recipients and messengers of this glorious reconciliation, entrusted with the sacred task of proclaiming this message of new creation to others.

During the Video

No Blessings without the Person

- Why is the concept of the golden chain helpful? What is missing from this concept?

  The golden chain of Romans 8:29–30 outlines the steps of salvation in a logical order: God's election leads to regeneration, which leads to faith, which leads to justification, which leads to sanctification, which leads to perseverance in faith, which leads to glory. This chain can be very helpful to a believer's understanding of the sequential order in which redemption is applied to God's elect. The golden chain, however, makes no explicit reference to the person of Jesus Christ. When Christians think only in terms of the blessings of the gospel without rooting these blessings in Christ, they run the risk of divorcing the gospel from the One who is the gospel.

- How does 1 Corinthians 6:15–20 reveal the power of a believer's union with Christ?

  When Paul addresses the problem of prostitution and adultery among the Corinthian believers, he makes a powerful statement about a believer's union with Christ. He points out that because Christians are joined to Christ, a believer who engages in physical acts of sin brings Christ into those sins. This passage therefore demonstrates that Christians are united to Christ to such an extent that Christ is present with them in all that they do.

Three Dimensions of Our Union

- What are the three major aspects of union with Christ?

  Dr. Ferguson explained that a believer's union with Christ is first of all grounded in God's eternal election. Second, it is grounded in Christ's incarnation. Third, it is grounded in the believer's act of bonding himself to Christ in faith.

- What do we know of Jesus' life between the ages of twelve and thirty? How does this knowledge enhance our understanding of His relationship with the Father?

  All that is known about the life of Christ between the ages of twelve and thirty is that he "increased in wisdom and in stature and in favor with God and man" (Luke 2:52). While growth in wisdom and stature are to be expected, it comes as a surprise to many Christians that Jesus grew in favor with God during these years. This verse therefore indicates that Jesus enjoyed a dynamic and increasingly mature relationship with His heavenly Father throughout His time on earth.

- What kind of vocabulary does Paul use to describe belief in Christ? How does this compare to other ancient Greek writings?

  When Paul writes in the New Testament about belief in Christ, he uses the term pisteuō eis, *which translates literally as "believe into." Nowhere else in all the literature of antiquity is there another instance of one person's "believing into" another person. Paul may have invented this unique phrase to underscore the point that faith in Christ brings the believer "into" Christ, allowing him to experience intimate union and communion with Him.*

After the Video

- How might Christians be in danger of focusing on the spiritual blessings that Christ offers without focusing on Christ Himself?

  Because the blessings that believers possess in Christ are so magnificent, our human nature can easily fixate on these blessings while our attention drifts away from the person of Christ, in whom we receive these blessings. Dr. Ferguson observes that a great deal of the religious teaching that is broadcast on the television and radio offers the benefits of Christ without offering Christ Himself. This is a dangerous practice that can lead to the neglect of the crucial relationship with Jesus, from whom all these blessings flow.

- What does it mean that a believer's union with Christ is experienced through faith but is not grounded in faith? How can this truth encourage Christians who falter?

  It is through faith that we are initially joined to Christ and become recipients of the rich blessings that flow from this union. Yet our status in Christ actually rests not on the strength of our faith but on the strength of Him in whom we place our faith. Believers who struggle with doubt can take heart that their union with Christ does not falter when their faith falters, because this union is grounded in God's eternal purpose.

- How does the reality of living in a different country from one's birth illustrate Paul's point in 2 Corinthians 5:17?

  Dr. Ferguson is originally from Scotland but has spent many years living in the United States. When asked what the difference is, he replies that absolutely everything is different in some way or another. In the same way, 2 Corinthians 5:17 teaches that when people become Christians, they take a step toward a new world order where everything is different in some way because of the transformative nature of being united to Jesus Christ.

REVIEW QUIZ

Lesson 3

1. **D.**
   A believer's union with Christ is grounded in God's eternal election, Christ's incarnation, and the believer's bonding of himself to Christ in faith. A person's union with Christ is not grounded in good works. Rather, good works and growth in personal holiness are one of the effects that come from being united to Christ.

2. **A.**
   A Christian's faith may falter, but that does not mean that his union with Christ will falter. Union with Christ is grounded not in the strength of a person's faith, but in the strength and purposes of the God in whom that faith is placed.

3. **C.**
   The grammar that Paul uses to describe faith in Jesus has no exact parallel in ancient Greco-Roman literature. Instead of saying "believe in Christ" or "believe on Christ," he consistently uses "believe into Christ" when he talks about having faith in Jesus.

4. **B.**
   There are many similarities between the union that a husband and wife experience and the union that believers experience with Jesus Christ. Yet it is more accurate to say that marriage is based on union with Christ than to say that union with Christ is based on marriage.

5. **A.**
   Dr. Ferguson translated the opening phrase in 2 Corinthians 5:17 as "If any in Christ, new creation." While most English translations fill in the gaps to say something to the effect of "If anyone is in Christ, he is a new creation," Dr. Ferguson argues that the intent of the text is not merely to say that the believer has been

made new but rather to proclaim that those who are in Christ have taken a step into a different world in which all things are being made new.

6. **B.**
   John Calvin described the vital importance of being united to Christ in his Institutes of the Christian Religion *when he wrote, "As long as Christ remains outside of us and we are separated from him, all that he has suffered and done for the salvation of the human race remains useless and of no value for us."*

4

Adam & Christ

INTRODUCTION

Before we become united by faith to Jesus Christ, we are already united by nature to Adam, the forefather of humanity. As Dr. Ferguson explains in this lesson, no person is a spiritual island. Every individual is united either to Adam or to Christ. Union with Adam leads to sin, despair, and death. Union with Christ leads to forgiveness, hope, and eternal life. Christ's offer to join Him in this new humanity is too important to ignore.

LEARNING GOALS

When you have finished this lesson, you should be able to:

- Explain how Romans 5:12–21 fits into the larger contexts of the book of Romans and human history
- Compare and contrast the characteristics, actions, and impact of Adam and Jesus Christ

KEY IDEAS

- The whole of human history depends on what two men have done—Adam, the first man, and our Lord Jesus Christ, the second man.
- Every human being is either united to Adam in sin or united to Christ in redemption.
- The second Adam, Jesus Christ, has succeeded where the first Adam failed.
- Just as Adam was the father of humanity, Jesus Christ has become the father of a new humanity.

REFLECTION & DISCUSSION QUESTIONS

Before the Video

What Do You Think?

Take a moment to answer the following questions. They will prepare you for the lecture.

- Who is an influential person that you know? How has this person affected the lives of others? Has this impact been mostly positive or negative?

- What do you think are some of the most important events in history? What have been some of the most important moments in your own life?

Scripture Reading

For if, because of one man's trespass, death reigned through that one man, much more will those who receive the abundance of grace and the free gift of righteousness reign in life through the one man Jesus Christ. Therefore, as one trespass led to condemnation for all men, so one act of righteousness leads to justification and life for all men. For as by the one man's disobedience the many were made sinners, so by the one man's obedience the many will be made righteous.

—Romans 5:17–19

- What are the results of the trespass committed by the first man, Adam? What are the results of the righteousness of Jesus Christ?

During the Video

Answer the following questions while you watch the video. They will guide you through the lecture.

The Larger Narrative *0:00–11:07*

- How does Romans 5:12–21 fit into the larger framework of the book of Romans?

- Which two human conditions are rooted in the lives of Adam and Christ? In what way does a person fit into the narrative of one man or the other?

Two Men, Two Actions, Two Results *11:07–23:18*

- In what way is Adam considered a father? In what way is Jesus considered a father?
- How did the second Adam reverse the work of the first Adam?

After the Video

Answer the following questions after you have finished the lecture. They will help you identify and summarize the major points.

- According to Dr. Ferguson, why has it become so common in our culture to make up one's own identity? How does Romans 5:12–21 address our cultural identity crisis?

  If you are in a group, have the members answer the following questions: What events, influences, or factors have most profoundly shaped your sense of who you are? How has your relationship with Jesus changed how you think about your identity?
- How does the example of earthly inheritance illustrate the importance of Adam and Christ in a person's spiritual life?

  If you are in a group, have the members identify something important to them that they have inherited. What aspect of your inheritance in Christ means the most to you?
- How does the way in which a jeweler displays a jewel illustrate the difference between the work of Adam and the work of Christ?

  If you are in a group, have the members answer the following question: In what circumstances have you most clearly beheld the dazzling beauty of Jesus Christ on display?

PRAYER

Commit what you have learned from God's Word in this lesson to prayer.

- Praise God for sending a second Adam, Jesus Christ, to redeem fallen ones of the first Adam.
- Confess areas of your life where you are most prone to seek an identity apart from Christ.

- Thank God for grounding your life in the overarching narrative of redemption in Jesus.
- Ask God to help you proclaim the good news of Jesus to someone who needs a lasting identity.

REVIEW QUIZ

Use these multiple-choice questions to measure what you learned from this lesson.

1. Romans 5:12–21 is best understood in which of the following ways?
   a. As a literary tangent that is unrelated to the rest of Romans
   b. As an appendix to Romans that provides extra background information
   c. As the center point of the first eight chapters of Romans
   d. As the thematic break between the first and second halves of Romans

2. Old Testament figures such as Abraham and David were saved not by their own righteousness but by faith.
   a. True
   b. False

3. What does Dr. Ferguson see as the source of the identity crisis that many people experience today?
   a. An excess of conflicting and confusing narratives
   b. Insufficient funds to help people discover a true identity
   c. Rejection of who Scripture says we are
   d. Lack of self-discovery

4. Which of the messianic titles in Isaiah 9:6 relates most closely to Romans 5:12–21?
   a. "Everlasting Father"
   b. "Mighty God"
   c. "Prince of Peace"
   d. "Wonderful Counselor"

5. To which person are all members of the human race naturally united?
   a. Abraham
   b. Adam
   c. Jesus
   d. Satan

6. Which great oratorio declares, "That flesh and blood which did in Adam fail, should strive afresh against the foe, should strive and should prevail"?
   a. *Messiah* by Handel
   b. *St. Matthew Passion* by Bach
   c. *The Creation* by Haydn
   d. *The Dream of Gerontius* by Elgar

Answer Key—Adam & Christ

REFLECTION & DISCUSSION QUESTIONS

Before the Video

What Do You Think?

These are personal questions. The answers should be based on your own knowledge and experience.

Scripture Reading

- What are the results of the trespass committed by the first man, Adam? What are the results of the righteousness of Jesus Christ?

  According to Romans 5:17–19, the trespass committed by Adam has resulted in a reign of death, such that all people bear the guilt of Adam's sin, are morally corrupt, commit sins themselves, and are therefore condemned. On the other hand, the righteousness of Jesus Christ has made the many righteous. Those who receive the abundance of grace and free gift of righteousness that Christ offers receive justification and life.

During the Video

The Larger Narrative

- How does Romans 5:12–21 fit into the larger framework of the book of Romans?

  In many ways, Romans 5:12–21 forms the center point of everything that Paul says in the first eight chapters of his letter to the Romans. Having described humanity's sinful condition and the Christian's justified condition in the first four and a half chapters, Paul takes a step back to explain how both are the result of the lives of two men. Having examined the ripple effects that both these men have sent through the human race, Paul builds on this foundation in the next three chapters to explain in greater detail the effects and dynamics of a believer's union with Christ.

- Which two human conditions are rooted in the lives of Adam and Christ? In what way does a person fit into the narrative of one man or the other?

  The moral state of humanity before God is rooted in the lives of two men, Adam and Christ. The sinful condition into which all people are born is the direct result of Adam's sin. In the same way, the justified condition into which believers enter by faith is the direct result of Christ's righteousness. Each person's life fits into the larger context of Adam's sinful condition or Christ's righteous condition. Without a clear grasp of the significance of these two moral representatives of the human race, a person will not understand the true significance or moral state of his own life.

Two Men, Two Actions, Two Results

- In what way is Adam considered a father? In what way is Jesus considered a father?

  As the first man, Adam was the spiritual head and moral representative of all humanity. He was the father of the entire human race in both a biological sense and a moral sense. As a result, his rebellion against God has severe consequences for all who belong to his family. The Son of God came into the world not simply as another isolated individual but to become the head or father of a new humanity. While it may seem counterintuitive to think of Jesus Christ as a father, Isaiah 9:6 foretold that the Messiah would be called "Everlasting Father." Although Jesus did not have any biological children, through His death and resurrection He became the spiritual father of a new humanity—those who have been born again and united to Him by faith.

- How did the second Adam reverse the work of the first Adam?

  In obedience to His heavenly Father, Jesus lived a perfect life of obedience to God's law and undid the disobedience of our first father, Adam. Where Adam failed, Jesus succeeded. Jesus' righteous life earned the righteous status in the Father's eyes that Adam and his descendants could never earn. Moreover, Jesus' atoning death on the cross paid the moral debt that Adam and his offspring could never pay. As a result, Jesus thoroughly reversed the work of the first man and has reconciled the human race to God.

After the Video

- According to Dr. Ferguson, why has it become so common in our culture to make up one's own identity? How does Romans 5:12–21 address our cultural identity crisis?

  Dr. Ferguson observed that it has become commonplace for individuals to invent their own distinct identity based solely on their own terms and desires. He pointed out that the underlying reason why people need to make up an identity of their own is that, at a fundamental level, they do not know who they are. In order to keep from living the kind of destabilized life that has become the norm in our day, people need to ground their lives in a larger narrative that spans the whole of history. Romans 5:12–21 helpfully summarizes this narrative, situating each person in the fallen narrative of Adam or the redemptive narrative of Jesus Christ.

- How does the example of earthly inheritance illustrate the importance of Adam and Christ in a person's spiritual life?

  Most people recognize intuitively and instinctively that there is something about the way we have been created that involves us in the lives of our parents and involves them in our lives. Our circumstances are profoundly shaped by things that we inherit from those who have gone before us, such as wealth, generational patterns of hardship, or genetic traits. In the same way, the spiritual inheritance that we receive either from Adam or from Jesus Christ will determine our eternal condition.

- How does the way in which a jeweler displays a jewel illustrate the difference between the work of Adam and the work of Christ?

  It is common for a jeweler to place a black cloth on the table while displaying a jewel to a customer. The luster of a jewel is seen most clearly against a dark background. The same is true of the gospel. Paul presents the work of Christ in contrast to the work of Adam because the dark background of Adam's sin and the resulting condemnation of the human race reveals the true beauty of Christ's redeeming work.

REVIEW QUIZ

Lesson 4

1. **C.**
   Romans 5:12–21 forms the center point of the first eight chapters of Romans. Everything Paul says up to 5:12–21 leads the reader to the foundation of the two lives of Adam and Christ. Everything from 5:12–21 onward leads the reader to the individual lives that result from this foundation.

2. **A.**
   When Paul teaches that salvation is by faith, he points out that Old Testament figures were also saved by faith, not by their own works (Rom. 4:2–3). This is a key point in his argument leading up to Romans 5:12–21.

3. **C.**
   Dr. Ferguson notes that most people today attempt to craft an identity and narrative for themselves because they lack a compelling overarching narrative to make sense of their lives. The fundamental reason for this, he argues, is that we have rejected the notion of who Scripture says we are. As a result, our culture is on a misguided quest to determine who we are on our own terms.

4. **A.**
   Though we are not accustomed to thinking of Jesus as a father, His fatherly role described in Romans 5:12–21 was prefigured in the title "Everlasting Father" that appears in Isaiah 9:6.

5. **B.**
   Since all people are Adam's posterity, we are by nature united to Adam as our progenitor and original moral representative. To be united to Christ requires the supernatural gift of faith.

6. **D.**
   Edward Elgar's great oratorio The Dream of Gerontius *recapitulates the message of Romans 5:12–21 when it declares, "That flesh and blood which did in Adam fail, should strive afresh against the foe, should strive and should prevail."*

5

A New Creation

INTRODUCTION

Scripture presents a stark contrast between the old creation into which each person is born through union with Adam and the new creation into which believers are born anew through union with Christ. In this lesson, Dr. Ferguson will describe ways that the old creation distorts human perceptions of Christ and others, and then he will explore some of the glorious realities of God's new creation.

LEARNING GOALS

When you have finished this lesson, you should be able to:

- Describe specific ways that sin has distorted human perceptions of God and one another
- Articulate the significance of reconciliation in Scripture and in the Christian life

KEY IDEAS

- Union with Christ liberates believers from sin's domain of distortion and darkness.
- Union with Christ brings about a new view of Jesus and other people.
- Union with Christ enables sinners to be reconciled to God.
- Union with Christ gives believers assurance that they will live in His presence forever.

REFLECTION & DISCUSSION QUESTIONS

Before the Video

What Do You Think?

Take a moment to answer the following questions. They will prepare you for the lecture.

- How would you describe your life before you came to know the Lord? What are some of the most significant changes that becoming a Christian has made in your life?

- How do people see you differently now that you are a follower of Jesus Christ? How do you see other people differently now that you are a follower of Christ?

Scripture Reading

Surely he has borne our griefs and carried our sorrows; yet we esteemed him stricken, smitten by God, and afflicted. But he was pierced for our transgressions; he was crushed for our iniquities; upon him was the chastisement that brought us peace, and with his wounds we are healed. All we like sheep have gone astray; we have turned—every one—to his own way; and the LORD has laid on him the iniquity of us all.

—Isaiah 53:4–6

- What effects of a believer's union with Christ are described in this passage?

During the Video

Answer the following questions while you watch the video. They will guide you through the lecture.

The Distorted Old World *0:00–8:39*

- How does Dr. Ferguson describe the distortion that forms the background for the new creation in 2 Corinthians 5?

- How did the Corinthian believers regard other people before they knew Christ?

- How did the Corinthian believers regard Jesus before they knew Christ?

The New World Reconciled in Christ *8:39–23:13*

- How does Dr. Ferguson explain the concept of reconciliation?

- In what way did the Old Testament sacrifices represent an exchange?

- What kind of exchange takes place in the lives of believers as a result of their reconciliation to God in Christ?

After the Video

Answer the following questions after you have finished the lecture. They will help you identify and summarize the major points.

- What are the two different families to which Christians have belonged?

  If you are in a group, have the members discuss their answers to the following questions: How have you been blessed by belonging to Christ's family? In what ways can this family better support you in your new life in Christ? In what ways can you better support it?

- What happens if Christians forget where they came from in the Christian life?

  If you are in a group, have the members discuss how God's grace has made a difference in their lives. Invite them to respond to the following question: How would your life be different today if you did not know Jesus?

- What guiding question for the Christian life did Dr. Ferguson propose in this lesson? What can Christians do to carry out this principle more fully?

  If you are in a group, have the members share ideas about how they can please God in their everyday lives.

PRAYER

Commit what you have learned from God's Word in this lesson to prayer.

- Praise God for delivering you from the domain of sin's darkness and distortion.
- Confess lingering sinful tendencies that you bring with you into Christ's new world.
- Thank God that Jesus has taken your place as the sacrificial Lamb, offered once for all for sins.
- Ask God to help you regard Christ and your neighbors from an increasingly Spirit-filled point of view.

REVIEW QUIZ

Use these multiple-choice questions to measure what you learned from this lesson.

1. How does Paul describe the way that people view one another apart from Christ?
   a. "According to the flesh"
   b. "In a spirit of tolerance for sin"
   c. "Through the lens of divine judgment"
   d. "With sober judgment"

2. Which hymn expresses the truth that no amount of remorse for sin can ever atone for sin?
   a. "And Can It Be That I Should Gain"
   b. "Holy, Holy, Holy!"
   c. "Rock of Ages, Cleft for Me"
   d. "When I Survey the Wondrous Cross"

3. According to Dr. Ferguson, which of the following words best describes the meaning of the term *reconciliation*?
   a. "Change"
   b. "Exchange"
   c. "Peace"
   d. "Redemption"

4. The way of salvation in the Bible is always the way of exchange.
   a. True
   b. False

5. Which guiding question does Dr. Ferguson recommend for believers?
   a. "What feels right?"
   b. "What actions will bring me the most favor in the eyes of a holy God?"
   c. "What is most going to tend to the pleasure of my Lord Jesus Christ?"
   d. "What would Jesus do?"

6. What fundamental claim about Jesus does Hebrews 13:8 make?
   a. Jesus is eternal.
   b. Jesus never changes His mind when He decides to bring someone to faith.
   c. Jesus possesses the divine attribute of immutability.
   d. Jesus remains the same today as He was in the Gospels.

Answer Key—A New Creation

REFLECTION & DISCUSSION QUESTIONS

Before the Video

What Do You Think?

These are personal questions. The answers should be based on your own knowledge and experience.

Scripture Reading

- What effects of a believer's union with Christ are described in this passage?

  Isaiah 53:4–6 describes the great exchange that takes place between Christ and those who are united to Him by faith. Through our union with Him, Christ has borne our griefs and sorrows. Because He carried the guilt of human sin, He was afflicted and smitten by God as sinful humans deserve to be. Because He was pierced, crushed, and punished in our place, all who are united to Him experience spiritual healing and peace with God.

During the Video

The Distorted Old World

- How does Dr. Ferguson describe the distortion that forms the background for the new creation in 2 Corinthians 5?

  Just as a jewel looks brightest against the background of a dark cloth, Paul presents the distortion of human lives through the fall as the background to 2 Corinthians 5:17. In 2 Corinthians 4, he notes that the god of this age has blinded human minds to the gospel so that, although the glory of Christ is present in the gospel, sinners cannot behold it apart from God's grace.

- How did the Corinthian believers regard other people before they knew Christ?

  Paul notes in 2 Corinthians 5:16 that the Corinthian believers—as all fallen human beings do—regarded other people according to the flesh. The natural inclination of the sinful mind is to judge people according to worldly standards.

- How did the Corinthian believers regard Jesus before they knew Christ?

  Paul includes the statement in 2 Corinthians 5:16 that he and the Corinthian believers used to view Jesus according to the flesh. The tendency of sinful humanity is to view Him in merely human terms. Even if we respect Him as a teacher, our inclination is always to have the last word, to hold ourselves above Christ as the chief authority in our lives.

The New World Reconciled in Christ

- How does Dr. Ferguson explain the concept of reconciliation?

  Dr. Ferguson pointed out that the word reconciliation *essentially means "change" or "exchange." When believers are reconciled to God, their old relationship with Him is exchanged for a new one in Christ.*

- In what way did the Old Testament sacrifices represent an exchange?

  Even in the Old Testament, the way of salvation in the Bible is the way of exchange. In the Old Testament sacrificial system, God's people understood that they deserved to die, but that the animal being sacrificed was taking their place. This sacrificial system, in which animal sacrifices made provisional atonement for the sins of the people, pointed forward to Jesus Christ, who was the ultimate sacrificial Lamb, offered once and for all to atone for human sin.

- What kind of exchange takes place in the lives of believers as a result of their reconciliation to God in Christ?

  Just as believers exchange their sins for the righteousness of Christ when they place their faith in Him, they also experience a dramatic exchange in the way that they live. Those who are found in Christ exchange the old world for a new one. Once bound to sin, redeemed sinners exchange this old life for a new one in which their chief aim is to live for His glory, to honor and please Him in all areas of life.

After the Video

- What are the two different families to which Christians have belonged?

  By nature, we belong to the old family of Adam. By grace, we have been adopted into a new family in Christ. Although the old family no longer has a claim over us, it may take a long time for our old instincts to fade away, so we will likely bring many of sin's distortions with us into the new family. Nevertheless, Christ is working in us within the context of this new family to bring us more fully into His new creation.

- What happens if Christians forget where they came from in the Christian life?

  Dr. Ferguson pointed out that if we forget where we came from, we begin to take the grace of God very lightly. Our fallen human tendency is to downplay the severity of our own sin and therefore minimize the necessity of God's grace. Therefore, we must never lose sight of the backdrop of the distortion of sin in our lives and of the glory of the new creation that is taking place in us through Jesus Christ.

- What guiding question for the Christian life did Dr. Ferguson propose in this lesson? What can Christians do to carry out this principle more fully?

  Dr. Ferguson suggested that Christians can clear up 99 percent of life's choices by asking the question, "What, according to God's Word, is most going to tend to the pleasure of my Lord Jesus Christ?" In order to know what will bring the most pleasure to Christ, Christians should pursue greater knowledge of God's Word.

REVIEW QUIZ

Lesson 5

1. **A.**
Speaking to the Corinthian believers in 2 Corinthians 5:16, Paul instructs that from now on they are to "regard no one according to the flesh." This implies that the natural way that fallen people view one another is according to the flesh, assessing one another in terms of worldly characteristics and values.

2. **C.**
The beloved hymn "Rock of Ages, Cleft for Me" contains the statement "Could my zeal no respite know, could my tears forever flow, all for sin could not atone; thou must save, and thou alone." These words affirm the truth that atonement for sin comes not from an individual's good works or remorse for his sins but from the saving work of Christ alone.

3. **B.**
Dr. Ferguson described reconciliation as an exchange. Reconciliation means that a sinner who is united to Jesus Christ exchanges his old relationship with God for a new one in Christ.

4. **A.**
In both the Old Testament and New Testament, the idea of an exchange is central to redemption. In the Old Testament, this is seen in the sacrificial system, when animals were sacrificed for human sin. In the New Testament, this type of exchange is seen clearly in Jesus Christ, the ultimate sacrificial Lamb of God.

5. **C.**
Dr. Ferguson commended asking the question, "What, according to God's Word, is most going to tend to the pleasure of my Lord Jesus Christ?" as a guide for Christian living. Naturally, this approach implies that believers ought to know Scripture intimately in order to gain a better understanding of what is most pleasing to Him.

6. **D.**
Dr. Ferguson pointed out that when Hebrews 13:8 proclaims, "Jesus Christ is the same yesterday and today and forever," it is not making a statement that is primarily about Jesus' eternality, immutability, or resolve to save sinners. Rather, the intent of the author of Hebrews is most likely to affirm that Jesus is exactly the same today as He was in the Gospels. The Jesus that we know in the writings of Matthew, Mark, Luke, and John is the Jesus to whom we are united by faith.

6

Crucified with Christ

INTRODUCTION

One of the most dramatic aspects of becoming a disciple of Christ is the fact that He invites sinners to die to themselves in order to experience new life. Those who have become united to Christ experience a radically different way of being human because they have in fact died to their old selves and their sinful ways of living. In this lesson, Dr. Sinclair Ferguson explores the profound reality of being crucified with Christ.

LEARNING GOALS

When you have finished this lesson, you should be able to:

- Describe attributes of God's love and why Christians can be sure that God loves them
- Explain the significance of being crucified with Christ

KEY IDEAS

- Jesus, the Son of God, expressed His love by giving Himself for others (Gal. 2:20).
- Christians have been crucified with Christ, yet live in Him by faith.
- While Christians live in Christ, it is also true that Christ lives in them.

REFLECTION & DISCUSSION QUESTIONS

Before the Video

What Do You Think?

Take a moment to answer the following questions. They will prepare you for the lecture.

- How can people know that God loves them? Can God's love be measured? If so, how?

- What does it mean to be truly alive?

Scripture Reading

For through the law I died to the law, so that I might live to God. I have been crucified with Christ. It is no longer I who live, but Christ who lives in me. And the life I now live in the flesh I live by faith in the Son of God, who loved me and gave himself for me. I do not nullify the grace of God, for if righteousness were through the law, then Christ died for no purpose.

—Galatians 2:19–21

- How does Paul describe the believer's relationship to the law in these verses? How does he describe the life that believers now experience?

During the Video

Answer the following questions while you watch the video. They will guide you through the lecture.

Loved and Purchased by Christ *0:00–10:18*

- In what three ways can love be measured?

- How might Christians mistakenly measure Christ's love for them?

Crucified, yet Truly Alive *10:18–23:14*

- What three dimensions of faith does Reformed theology emphasize?

- What do the tense, voice, and mood of Paul's words in Galatians 2:20 communicate about what it means to be crucified with Christ?

- How is the old creation gone from the life of a believer?

After the Video

Answer the following questions after you have finished the lecture. They will help you identify and summarize the major points.

- How did Dr. Ferguson use the story of Cinderella to illustrate certain aspects of God's love?

  If you are in a group, have the members share ways of describing or thinking about God's love that they have found to be helpful.

- Is a believer's relationship with the Lord a fluid or constant reality? Explain.

  If you are in a group, have the members discuss how their own perception of God's love for them has changed over time. How is the reality of God's love presented in this lesson good news to you?

- How should the question "Who am I?" be answered by those who are united to Christ?

  If you are in a group, have the members discuss how their perception of their identity as disciples of Christ has changed or deepened as your group has journeyed through this teaching series.

PRAYER

Commit what you have learned from God's Word in this lesson to prayer.

- Praise God for redemption through His Son.
- Confess times when you have doubted God's love for you.
- Thank God for the Spirit's applying the benefits of Christ's death and resurrection to you.
- Ask God to give you greater assurance of His love for you and greater confidence in your status as a member of His new creation.

REVIEW QUIZ

Use these multiple-choice questions to measure what you learned from this lesson.

1. A Scripture passage's logic may differ from the order of its words.
   a. True
   b. False

2. Which of the following theologians wondered whether God loved His redeemed more than His Son because He sent His Son to die for them?
   a. B.B. Warfield
   b. Charles Spurgeon
   c. John Bunyan
   d. Martin Luther

3. Which of the following sustains a believer?
   a. A believer's faith
   b. A believer's good works
   c. The object of a believer's faith
   d. God's Word

4. What banishes the old creation from a Christian's life?
   a. Participation in the body of Christ
   b. Spiritual disciplines
   c. Union with a crucified Lord
   d. Vigorous efforts to put the sinful nature to death

5. What enables believers to say with the Apostle Paul, "Christ lives in me"?
   a. Assent
   b. Knowledge
   c. The Holy Spirit
   d. The sacraments

6. All *except* which of the following are the believer's answers to the question, "Who am I?"
   a. Someone in whom Christ lives
   b. Someone who can find evidence of God's love in his quality of life
   c. Someone who has been crucified with Christ
   d. Someone who is alive in Christ

Answer Key—Crucified with Christ

REFLECTION & DISCUSSION QUESTIONS

Before the Video

What Do You Think?

These are personal questions. The answers should be based on your own knowledge and experience.

Scripture Reading

- How does Paul describe the believer's relationship to the law in these verses? How does he describe the life that believers now experience?

  Paul describes the believer's relationship to the law as part of the old world that Christians leave behind when they become joined to Christ. Paul declares that he has died to the law so that he could now live to God. He also states that if righteousness could have been earned through the law, then there would have been no reason for Jesus to die on behalf of sinners. Since Paul and his fellow believers have been crucified with Jesus, they now live a new kind of life by faith. Indeed, their lives are now characterized by the reality that Jesus now dwells in them.

During the Video

Loved and Purchased by Christ

- In what three ways can love be measured?

  One way to measure love is by the greatness of the lover, and there is no greater lover than Jesus Christ. A second way to measure love is by the difference or distance between the lover and the loved one. Because Jesus is so great and fallen humans are so lowly, His love for His people is vast and overwhelming. A third way to measure love is by what the lover will do for the loved one. Because Christ loved His people to the extent that He was willing to die in their place, we know that His love is boundless and selfless.

- How might Christians mistakenly measure Christ's love for them?

  The natural human tendency is to gauge God's love by how well life is going. When things are going well, we take it as evidence that God loves us. When we encounter difficulty in life, we tend to question His love, yet the Bible never tells Christians to trust Jesus' love for them on the basis of everyday experience. Rather, it invites them to recognize that Jesus loves them because He willingly gave Himself for them.

Crucified, yet Truly Alive

- What three dimensions of faith does Reformed theology emphasize?

  Reformed theologians have traditionally described faith as a combination of three dimensions. The first dimension is knowledge. Someone cannot believe what he does not know. The second dimension is assent, because one cannot believe something that his mind rejects. The third dimension is trust. Faith is entrusting oneself to Christ, receiving and resting on Him alone for salvation.

- What do the tense, voice, and mood of Paul's words in Galatians 2:20 communicate about what it means to be crucified with Christ?

  When Paul says, "I have been crucified with Christ," the tense, voice, and mood that he uses are of vital importance. Paul's use of the present tense indicates that this act of being crucified has already taken place and is therefore an established reality. Paul speaks of this reality in the passive voice, which implies that this is something that happens to believers; there is nothing they need to do in order to bring it about. Finally, Paul's use of the indicative mood confirms that no action is required of the believer. Rather, Paul invites Christians to recognize who they already are in Christ Jesus.

- How is the old creation gone from the life of a believer?

  Part of what it means to be united to Christ is that the old creation that believers formerly belonged to is no longer part of their lives. When a person is united to Christ, he is united to a crucified Christ. As a result, the Christian now shares in all the implications of that crucifixion. Because Christ died to the old world and was raised to the new world, all who are united to Him share in this exchange of realities.

After the Video

- How did Dr. Ferguson use the story of Cinderella to illustrate certain aspects of God's love?

  The story of Cinderella illustrates the greatness of the lover and the vast distance between the lover and the beloved. Because it is the prince who falls in love with Cinderella, the prince's royal blood and exalted station make his love significant and valuable. Moreover, the fact that such a royal figure would love a girl of lowly station such as Cinderella makes the prince's love overwhelming. In the same way, the all-surpassing greatness of Jesus Christ, contrasted with our natural state of spiritual poverty, reveals the boundless and beautiful nature of Christ's love for His church.

- Is a believer's relationship with the Lord a fluid or constant reality? Explain.

  We tend to assume that our relationship with the Lord is a fluid reality that ebbs and flows based on our good works or lack thereof. Dr. Ferguson offered a corrective to this way of thinking by affirming that a believer's relationship with Christ is rooted not in our personal holiness or intimacy with Jesus but in the fact that we are united with Him. Therefore, nothing can change the reality of who we are in Him.

- How should the question "Who am I?" be answered by those who are united to Christ?

  The Christian's answer to the question "Who am I?" is "I am somebody who has been crucified with Christ and also someone in whom that crucified, risen, ascended, and reigning Christ by His Holy Spirit indwells. I've been crucified with Christ and yet I live; and yet not I, but Christ lives in me."

REVIEW QUIZ

Lesson 6

1. **A.**
   Paul's words in Galatians 2:20 are "I have been crucified with Christ. It is no longer I who live, but Christ who lives in me. And the life I now live in the flesh I live by faith in the Son of God, who loved me and gave himself for me." But the logical flow of this statement is (1) "The Son of God loved me and gave Himself for me"; (2) "I live by faith in the Son of God"; (3) "I have been crucified with Christ, yet I live"; and "At the same time, it is also true that Christ lives in me."

2. **B.**
   Dr. Ferguson pointed out that Charles Haddon Spurgeon marveled that, in light of the cross, it is almost as if the Father loves believers more than He loves His Son because of the great price of His Son, who purchased their redemption. This idea is not to be seriously entertained, but it does drive home the point of how amazing God's love is in sending His own Son on our behalf.

3. **C.**
   Dr. Ferguson affirmed that it is not a Christian's faith, works, or spiritual experience that sustains him. Rather, it is Jesus Christ, the object of the believer's faith, who causes the believer to stand.

4. **C.**
   Union with Christ is the gateway to living in a new reality. The old creation is gone and no longer has a claim over a believer because he is now united to a crucified Lord and shares in all the implications of Jesus' crucifixion.

5. **C.**
   When the Holy Spirit brings believers out of themselves and into Christ, the Spirit also comes to dwell within them. The Spirit dwells within God's people as the Spirit of the Lord Jesus, so that believers are able to say, as Paul does, that Christ lives in them.

6. **B.**
   The Christian's new identity includes being crucified with Christ, living in Christ, and having Christ dwell within him. A Christian's identity or status in God's eyes is not measured by how good or bad his life is but by the fact that Christ gave Himself up on the cross on his behalf.

7

Baptized into Christ

INTRODUCTION

"If God forgives by grace, why should I not sin?" This question has resurfaced in various forms since the time of Paul. His response to antinomianism—this idea that righteous living is optional for Christians—is rooted in the doctrine of union with Christ. In the last lesson, the far-reaching implications of being crucified with Christ were examined. In this lesson, Dr. Ferguson explains how we are united to Christ's death and also how we are united to His resurrection life through baptism.

LEARNING GOALS

When you have finished this lesson, you should be able to:

- Explain why the topic of continuing sin that Paul addresses in Romans 6 is important
- Summarize Paul's response to the issue of remaining sin in the life of a believer

KEY IDEAS

- Through baptism, Christians have been baptized into Christ's death and resurrection.
- Baptism is one of the ways that the Bible tells Christians who they are in Christ.
- It is illogical and absurd for those who have been baptized into a new reality to live according to the old reality.

REFLECTION & DISCUSSION QUESTIONS

Before the Video

What Do You Think?

Take a moment to answer the following questions. They will prepare you for the lecture.

- How important do you think it is for Christians to live holy lives? Explain your answer.

- When were you baptized? What significance does your baptism in the past have for your life today?

Scripture Reading

> *What shall we say then? Are we to continue in sin that grace may abound? By no means! How can we who died to sin still live in it? Do you not know that all of us who have been baptized into Christ Jesus were baptized into his death? We were buried therefore with him by baptism into death, in order that, just as Christ was raised from the dead by the glory of the Father, we too might walk in newness of life.*
>
> —Romans 6:1–4

- Building on the previous lesson's theme of being crucified with Christ, how does union with Christ's death and resurrection affect the way that Christians are to live now?

During the Video

Answer the following questions while you watch the video. They will guide you through the lecture.

Romans 6: The Challenge *0:00–11:37*

- What was the Apostle Paul accused of teaching in Romans 6:1? In what way did the Reformers face a similar accusation?

- How does Dr. Ferguson summarize Paul's overall response to the question raised in Romans 6:1?

Paul's First Response: Emotion *11:37–15:31*

- What is the first thing Paul says in response to the question raised in Romans 6:1? How does this response involve his emotions?

- According to Dr. Ferguson, how does the gospel relate to a Christian's thoughts and emotions?

Paul's Second Response: Explanation *15:31–23:14*

- In what two ways do people usually speak of their baptism? What is missing from these approaches?

- How does Dr. Ferguson sum up Paul's argument about baptism in Romans 6?

After the Video

Answer the following questions after you have finished the lecture. They will help you identify and summarize the major points.

- How did Dr. Ferguson describe the appropriate role of emotions in the Christian life?

  If you are in a group, have the members discuss opinions about the role of faith and emotions that they have found to be helpful or not so helpful.

- How does the cognitive and emotional growth of a child illustrate truths about a Christian's growth in Christ?

  If you are in a group, have the members discuss which aspect of their faith— their knowledge or their emotions—tends to lead them.

- How did Dr. Ferguson use an example from his personal experience to explain Paul's reaction in Romans 6? What does this illustration communicate about Paul's immediate reaction?

  If you are in a group, have the members identify and share a key insight from this lesson that can help clarify their identity in Christ Jesus.

PRAYER

Commit what you have learned from God's Word in this lesson to prayer.

- Praise God for the clear answers in Scripture to who you are and how you should live.

- Confess any ways that you tend to neglect mental or emotional aspects of your faith.
- Thank God for giving you a new name and identity through your baptism into Christ.
- Ask God to help you live in accordance with the reality of who you are in Jesus Christ.

REVIEW QUIZ

Use these multiple-choice questions to measure what you learned from this lesson.

1. Which of the following preachers remarked that he would not preach on the book of Romans until he understood Romans 6?
   a. Charles Haddon Spurgeon
   b. D. Martyn Lloyd-Jones
   c. John Bunyan
   d. Martin Luther

2. Paul's response to the accusation of antinomianism in Romans 6 includes all *except* which of the following?
   a. Emotion
   b. Explanation
   c. Exposition
   d. Evaluation

3. According to the King James Version, what is Paul's response in Romans 6:2 to the question raised in 6:1?
   a. "By no means!"
   b. "Certainly not!"
   c. "God forbid."
   d. "May it never be!"

4. Which of the following preachers was said to have had "Bibline" blood?
   a. Charles Haddon Spurgeon
   b. D. Martyn Lloyd-Jones
   c. John Bunyan
   d. Martin Luther

5. According to Dr. Ferguson, how should a Christian's understanding of the gospel relate to his emotional life?
   a. Cognitive engagement of the gospel is to be emphasized over emotional engagement.
   b. Emotional engagement of the gospel is to be emphasized over cognitive engagement.
   c. Mental and emotional engagement of the gospel takes place simultaneously.
   d. Renewal of the mind leads to transformation of the heart.

6. In the New Testament, baptism represents a naming ceremony.
   a. True
   b. False

Answer Key—Baptized into Christ

REFLECTION & DISCUSSION QUESTIONS

Before the Video

What Do You Think?

These are personal questions. The answers should be based on your own knowledge and experience.

Scripture Reading

- Building on the previous lesson's theme of being crucified with Christ, how does union with Christ's death and resurrection affect the way that Christians are to live now?

  Because Christians have been crucified and buried with Christ through baptism, we have died to sin. We have now been raised with Christ to a new life, in which sin no longer has a claim on us. Therefore, the very idea of continuing to live in sin is contrary to the new reality that Christians inhabit as a result of being united to the Lord Jesus.

During the Video

Romans 6: The Challenge

- What was the Apostle Paul accused of teaching in Romans 6:1? In what way did the Reformers face a similar accusation?

  In Romans 6:1, Paul raises the question whether a Christian should sin so that the grace of God might abound all the more. Although he raises this question hypothetically in this passage, he mentions earlier in Romans 3:8 that some had accused him of advocating this position, known as antinomianism. Interestingly, Reformers such as Martin Luther and John Calvin also faced this accusation from people who feared that the Reformation emphasis on salvation by grace alone through faith alone in Christ alone would prompt people to live lives of moral licentiousness.

- How does Dr. Ferguson summarize Paul's overall response to the question raised in Romans 6:1?

  In essence, Paul responds that those who consider God's grace to be a license to go on sinning do not understand what it means to be baptized. When Jesus was baptized in the Jordan, He was baptized into the sins of His people; when believers are baptized into Christ, they are baptized into His righteousness. In short, Paul contends that it is not logically possible to be baptized into Christ's righteousness and then go on living as though one were still under the domination of sin. In this lesson and the next, Dr. Ferguson presents Paul's response, using the topics of emotion, explanation, exposition, implication, and exhortation.

Paul's First Response: Emotion

- What is the first thing Paul says in response to the question raised in Romans 6:1? How does this response involve his emotions?

  Paul's initial statement in response to the error of antinomianism expressed in Romans 6:1 is direct and succinct. He retorts, "By no means!"—or, as the King James Version translates it, "God forbid." He instinctively recoils from the mere suggestion that Christians ought to go on sinning.

- According to Dr. Ferguson, how does the gospel relate to a Christian's thoughts and emotions?

  Dr. Ferguson alluded to Charles Spurgeon's remark that if John Bunyan, the Nonconformist preacher and author of The Pilgrim's Progress, *had been pricked, he would have bled "Bibline" blood. This is a creative way of pointing out that over the course of a lifetime, the gospel not only brings clarity to a Christian's thinking but also touches and shapes believers at a deep emotional level. As Scripture demonstrates, the renewal of the Apostle Paul's mind also led to the cleansing and transforming of his emotional life by the power of the gospel.*

Paul's Second Response: Explanation

- In what two ways do people usually speak of their baptism? What is missing from these approaches?

  When asked about the meaning of their baptism, most people say something like this: "It was something done to me when I was just a baby" or "I professed my faith and was baptized at this particular time in my life." What is missing from both these approaches to thinking about baptism is the fact that they focus on what the individual or the individual's parents did rather than on what God did through the act of baptism.

- How does Dr. Ferguson sum up Paul's argument about baptism in Romans 6?

  Paul's discussion of baptism in Romans 6 can essentially be summed up as follows: "If that's who you are, then live like that." Specifically, if someone has been baptized into Christ's death and resurrection, he should live like it.

After the Video

- How did Dr. Ferguson describe the appropriate role of emotions in the Christian life?

  Dr. Ferguson observed that Christians are rightly taught not to live their Christian lives on the basis of emotion. Spiritual renewal comes not by a change in one's emotions but from a change in one's understanding. Yet believers must not forget that when Paul speaks in Romans 12:2 about the renewing of the mind leading to a transformed life, he is not speaking only about cognitive renewal. Rather, the gospel penetrates a person's life to transform his thoughts, emotions, and desires to more closely resemble those of Jesus.

- How does the cognitive and emotional growth of a child illustrate truths about a Christian's growth in Christ?

  As children grow, they develop at both a cognitive level and an emotional level. In the current information age, many parents may observe that their children develop a large knowledge base quickly, but that their emotional base may lag far behind. A person will not reach maturity while a significant disconnect remains between the extent of his growth in knowledge and the extent of his growth as a person. In the same way, Christians whose experience of faith is overwhelmingly cognitive or emotional will experience an imbalance in their relationship with the Lord.

- How did Dr. Ferguson use an example from his personal experience to explain Paul's reaction in Romans 6? What does this illustration communicate about Paul's immediate reaction?

  Dr. Ferguson recounted the time when he was asked why he had not become an American citizen. His knee-jerk reaction was, "Because I'm Scottish!" Just as it would seem absurd for Dr. Ferguson to act in a manner that was contrary to his citizenship, so too Paul argues that it is absurd for a Christian to act contrary to his citizenship in Christ by living as though he were still under the dominion of sin.

REVIEW QUIZ

Lesson 7

1. **B.**
   Martyn Lloyd-Jones, arguably the greatest British preacher of the twentieth century, responded to an inquiry about when he would preach through the book of Romans by saying that he would begin to do so once he understood Romans 6.

2. **D.**
   Paul's response to the charge of antinomianism—referred to in Romans 3:8 and again in Romans 6:1—includes the elements of emotion, explanation, exposition, implication, and exhortation.

3. **C.**
   Of the various translations of Paul's response in Romans 6:2 that appear in English Bibles, perhaps the most vigorous and colorful expression of Paul's words appears in the King James Version's translation, "God forbid."

4. **C.**
   Writing in the late nineteenth century, the English preacher Charles Haddon Spurgeon said of the seventeenth-century Nonconformist preacher John Bunyan, "Prick him anywhere—his blood is Bibline, the very essence of the Bible flows from him."

5. **D.**
   A believer's experience of the gospel should be neither purely cognitive nor purely emotional, with one being emphasized over the other. As Romans 12:2 indicates, a mental understanding of the gospel that takes place by the renewing of one's mind ought to lead to a transformation of the heart and all other aspects of a believer's life.

6. **A.**
   The New Testament presents baptism as a type of naming ceremony. Someone who is united to Christ is taken out of the name he had, is placed in God's family, and receives a new name.

8

Set Free from Sin

INTRODUCTION

The sixth chapter of Paul's letter to the Romans deals with the important topic of the Christian's relationship with sin in light of God's grace. In the previous lesson, Dr. Ferguson presented two components of Paul's response to the challenge of antinomianism. In this lesson, Dr. Ferguson will continue to explore Paul's reaction to this issue by examining Paul's exposition, implication, and exhortation to the church in Romans 6. For those in Rome and for each of us today, Paul's message is clear: do not allow sin to reign any longer, but live a new life as someone who belongs to Christ.

LEARNING GOALS

When you have finished this lesson, you should be able to:

- Summarize Paul's exposition of the believer's new status in Romans 6:5–10
- Explain the implication of being united to Christ that appears in Romans 6:11
- Describe how Paul exhorts Christians to live in light of the gospel in Romans 6:12–14

KEY IDEAS

- Because believers have been crucified and raised with Christ, sin no longer has a claim over them.
- Because sin's reign over believers has been broken, believers are to think of themselves differently, as people who are free from sin.
- Because believers are to think of themselves as people who are free from sin, they are to renounce areas of sin in their lives and present themselves to God for righteousness.

REFLECTION & DISCUSSION QUESTIONS

Before the Video

What Do You Think?

Take a moment to answer the following questions. They will prepare you for the lecture.

- What are some of the main commitments and obligations in your life? What does it take for a person to be released from an obligation?

- How reliable are feelings as a guide to knowing what is true? Explain your answer.

Scripture Reading

Let not sin therefore reign in your mortal body, to make you obey its passions. Do not present your members to sin as instruments for unrighteousness, but present yourselves to God as those who have been brought from death to life, and your members to God as instruments for righteousness. For sin will have no dominion over you, since you are not under law but under grace.

—Romans 6:12–14

- How do these verses demonstrate the contrast between the two different worlds to which people can belong?

During the Video

Answer the following questions while you watch the video. They will guide you through the lecture.

Paul's Third Response: Exposition *0:00–16:04*

- What three basic truths does Paul present about a Christian's death to sin?

- What does Paul mean when he mentions the "body of death" in Romans 7:24?

- Why, according to Romans 6:6–7, are Christians no longer enslaved to sin? How does Dr. Ferguson suggest that this should be understood?

Paul's Fourth and Fifth Responses: Implication and Exhortation *16:04–23:00*

- What implication of being united to Jesus in baptism does Paul mention in Romans 6:11?

- How does Paul exhort believers to live in response to his teaching in Romans 6?

After the Video

Answer the following questions after you have finished the lecture. They will help you identify and summarize the major points.

- In what two ways have believers already been set free from sin? In what way are believers still waiting to be set free?

  If you are in a group, have the members discuss their understanding of being free in Christ. In what ways have you personally experienced freedom in Christ? What is an area of your life where you desire to see sin no longer dominate?

- How does Dr. Ferguson use his citizenship as an illustration of how the Christian is no longer under sin's dominion?

  If you are in a group, have the members consider other ways of illustrating the release of sin by using metaphors that are common to everyday life.

- How should Christians respond to their sense of not feeling dead to sin?

  If you are in a group, have the members identify a biblical truth that they have struggled to feel is true. How does this lesson change the way you think about this particular issue?

PRAYER

Commit what you have learned from God's Word in this lesson to prayer.

- Praise God for setting you free from the guilt and dominion of sin.
- Confess ways that you struggle to accept the Bible's teachings as true.
- Thank God for setting you free from sin even when you do not feel it to be true.
- Ask God to help you renounce sin's claim over your life.

REVIEW QUIZ

Use these multiple-choice questions to measure what you learned from this lesson.

1. Which of the following best describes what Paul means when he talks about the "old man" or "old self" in Romans 6:6?
   a. Believers who possess a level of spiritual maturity that comes with age
   b. Specific sins that Christians committed before they knew Christ
   c. The fallen, sinful order to which Christians used to belong
   d. Violence that Paul committed against Christians when he was a Pharisee

2. The word Paul uses to talk about being "set free" from sin in Romans 6:7 also means which of the following?
   a. "To baptize"
   b. "To justify"
   c. "To rename"
   d. "To renounce"

3. Which of the following best describes the current state of a believer's freedom from sin?
   a. Free from sin's guilt and presence
   b. Free from sin's presence and reign
   c. Free from sin's presence, guilt, and reign
   d. Free from sin's reign and guilt

4. Although Christians are not yet free from sin's reign, they can still experience small victories by choosing not to sin in certain situations.
   a. True
   b. False

5. Which of the following best describes the main thrust of Paul's accountancy language in Romans 6:11?
   a. "Make this up about yourself."
   b. "Reckon this to be true because it is true."
   c. "This is true of some Christians, but not of others."
   d. "Work yourself up to this."

6. A widespread misconception in the Christian church is that there is so much grace in Jesus Christ that there are no commands left for the believer to follow.
   a. True
   b. False

Answer Key—Set Free from Sin

REFLECTION & DISCUSSION QUESTIONS

Before the Video

What Do You Think?

These are personal questions. The answers should be based on your own knowledge and experience.

Scripture Reading

- How do these verses demonstrate the contrast between the two different worlds to which people can belong?

  After exhorting the believers in Rome not to allow sin to reign in their bodies, Paul contrasts the old way of living with the new way of living. In the old world, sin exercises dominion over fallen individuals, who therefore present their bodies to sin as instruments to be used in unrighteous pursuits. On the other hand, those who inhabit the new world have been brought from death to life and therefore live under grace instead of under the law. As a result of this change, believers are called to present their bodies to God as instruments for righteousness.

During the Video

Paul's Third Response: Exposition

- What three basic truths does Paul present about a Christian's death to sin?

  In response to the teaching that Christians are united to Christ's death and resurrection through their baptism, Paul presents three basic truths about the new status of those who are united to Jesus. First, the old man, or former self, has been crucified with Christ. Second, this happened so that the body of sin might be destroyed. Third, as a result, believers are no longer enslaved to sin.

- What does Paul mean when he mentions the "body of death" in Romans 7:24?

  When Paul mentions the "body of death," he is referring to the physical body that is dominated by death and that will one day die. He is also expressing the truth that before believers are found in Christ, their physical bodies are dominated by sin. Every aspect of a person—body, mind, spirit, and emotions—is born into the old order of sin and is in need of Christ's redemptive power.

- Why, according to Romans 6:6–7, are Christians no longer enslaved to sin? How does Dr. Ferguson suggest that this should be understood?

  According to Paul, the Christian's union with Christ's death is the key to freedom from sin. He points out in Romans 6:7 that one who has died has been "set free" from sin. Dr. Ferguson suggests that the Greek verb dikaioō *is best understood in this instance to mean that a Christian is now released from all obligations to sin that he once had.*

Paul's Fourth and Fifth Responses: Implication and Exhortation

- What implication of being united to Jesus in baptism does Paul mention in Romans 6:11?

  The implication of Paul's teaching is that those who are united to Christ must now consider themselves dead to sin and alive to God. Because God has decisively brought them into a new reality in Christ, they must live no longer as citizens of the old world but as citizens of the new world.

- How does Paul exhort believers to live in response to his teaching in Romans 6?

  Paul's concluding exhortation to the Christians in Rome is to no longer allow sin to reign in their bodies. Sin was the cruel old master, and Christians now serve a new and righteous master. Paul therefore exhorts them to renounce any claim that sin once had over them.

After the Video

- In what two ways have believers already been set free from sin? In what way are believers still waiting to be set free?

  Dr. Ferguson describes three dimensions of freedom from sin. First, believers have been set free from the guilt of sin as a result of justification by grace alone through faith alone in Christ alone. Second, the double cure of the gospel is that believers are also set free from sin's reign over them. Sin no longer dominates; believers have the opportunity to live a new life in Christ. Third, believers will one day be set free from the presence of sin in the new heaven and the new earth. Until then, we dwell in a world that continues to be tainted by sin's influence, but our citizenship is in heaven.

- How does Dr. Ferguson use his citizenship as an illustration of how the Christian is no longer under sin's dominion?

  Although Dr. Ferguson made it clear in the previous lesson that he has no intention of renouncing his Scottish citizenship, he indulges in a hypothetical scenario to illustrate the principle of citizenship and obligation. Suppose he has become an American citizen, and the Queen of England writes him a letter commanding him to fulfill certain obligations to the United Kingdom. Dr. Ferguson would write a response informing her that he is no longer under her dominion and therefore has no obligation to serve her in any way. This playful scenario illustrates Paul's point in Romans 6 that Christians do not owe sin anything. We have become citizens of a new kingdom, with the result that sin's former claims over us are null and void.

- How should Christians respond to their sense of not feeling dead to sin?

  Dr. Ferguson observed that often people struggle to feel that certain things the Bible says are true. Yet the truth of a matter does not rest on how we feel about it. Our feelings about whether something in the Bible is true are irrelevant. The reality and implications of Christ's death are not made true because of our feelings. His death is a historical reality that the gospel proclaims to be true. By God's grace, Christians come to feel the truth of Scripture gradually as the Spirit applies the gospel to their minds and hearts over time.

REVIEW QUIZ

Lesson 8

1. **C.**
   When Paul talks about the "old man" or "old self" in Romans 6:6, he is thinking back to what he said in chapter 5 about how Christians were once united by nature to Adam and to the fallen, sinful order that Adam's sin brought about.

2. **B.**
   The Greek verb translated "set free" in Romans 6:7 is dikaioō, *which is usually translated as a form of the verb "to justify" throughout the New Testament.*

3. **D.**
   Dr. Ferguson observed that those who are united to Christ have already been set free from sin's guilt and reign. Christians will not be free of the presence of sin, however, until Christ returns to consummate His new creation in the new heaven and new earth.

4. **B.**
   As the Apostle Paul points out in Romans 6, Christians are already free from sin's reign. This freedom is what enables believers not to sin. Until a person is free from the reign of sin over him, he has no choice but to sin.

5. **B.**
   Paul utilizes a verb associated with accounting when he exhorts the believers in Romans 6:11. This accountancy term carries with it the sense of "This is the truth; reckon it to be true, and depend on it because it is true."

6. **A.**
   Dr. Ferguson observes that many Christians consider God's grace in Christ to mean that biblical imperatives no longer apply to Christians. To the contrary, it is because of the greatness of God's grace in the gospel that Paul calls Christians to the most demanding imperatives imaginable in Romans 6:12–14.

9

Hidden in Christ

INTRODUCTION

Even after being united to Jesus Christ, Christians continue to experience struggles in their faith and lives. But ongoing struggles in the Christian life are not evidence of any deficiency in the power of the gospel; rather, they indicate a need for the gospel to take root more deeply in our hearts and minds. In this lesson, Dr. Ferguson celebrates the reality that all the riches of the gospel are already ours in Christ and have the power to release a decisive ripple effect in our identity, mentality, and destiny.

LEARNING GOALS

When you have finished this lesson, you should be able to:

- Summarize the false teaching that arose in the Colossian church and Paul's response to it
- Describe the new identity, mentality, and destiny that Christians enjoy in Jesus Christ

KEY IDEAS

- United to Christ, believers possess a new identity that is hidden with Christ in God.
- United to Christ, believers possess a new mentality, seeking things that are above.
- United to Christ, believers possess a new destiny, and when Jesus appears they will appear with Him and be like Him.

REFLECTION & DISCUSSION QUESTIONS

Before the Video

What Do You Think?

Take a moment to answer the following questions. They will prepare you for the lecture.

- What are some things you have seen Christians do in pursuit of a more meaningful Christian life? What seems to work, and what doesn't work?

- Who are some of the most spiritually mature Christians you know? Do they tend to be in the spotlight, or do they usually go unnoticed by most people?

Scripture Reading

Therefore, as you received Christ Jesus the Lord, so walk in him, rooted and built up in him and established in the faith, just as you were taught, abounding in thanksgiving. See to it that no one takes you captive by philosophy and empty deceit, according to human tradition, according to the elemental spirits of the world, and not according to Christ.

—Colossians 2:6–8

- According to this passage, how can someone who is united to Christ strengthen that union? What dangers are mentioned?

During the Video

Answer the following questions while you watch the video. They will guide you through the lecture.

A New Identity *0:00–13:56*

- How did false teaching likely begin and spread in the Colossian church?

- How did Paul respond to the false teaching in Colossae? How did he diagnose the Colossians' actual spiritual problem?

- What benefits are implied by Paul's summary of union with Christ in Colossians 3:1–4?

A New Mentality and a New Destiny *13:56–23:14*

- What question is Dr. Ferguson known to ask candidates during job interviews? What does the answer to this question reveal about a person?

- How does Dr. Ferguson say that Christians will appear at Christ's return?

After the Video

Answer the following questions after you have finished the lecture. They will help you identify and summarize the major points.

- How did the Colossian false teachers' view of the fullness of Christ compare with Paul's description of the fullness of Christ?

  If you are in a group, have the members identify ways that the contemporary church drifts into the habit of looking to practices and things rather than union with Christ to bring fullness to a believer's life.
- Why would Jesus consider Himself incomplete without His people?

  If you are in a group, have the members read Ephesians 5:25–30. How is Christ's love for the church and commitment to the church displayed in these verses?
- What story played a part in Dr. Ferguson's conversion to Jesus Christ? How does the person in that story illustrate the significance of union with Christ?

  If you are in a group, have the members describe the circumstances or factors that God used to bring them into a relationship with Jesus Christ.

PRAYER

Commit what you have learned from God's Word in this lesson to prayer.

- Praise God for giving you a new life and a new identity hidden with Christ.
- Confess ways that you have sought fullness of life apart from Jesus Christ.
- Thank God that all the fullness of the Christian life is already yours through the gospel.
- Ask God to help you cultivate greater intimacy with His Son, that you may enjoy your union with Him more and more.

REVIEW QUIZ

Use these multiple-choice questions to measure what you learned from this lesson.

1. To what does Dr. Ferguson compare reading certain New Testament letters?
   a. Deciphering a complex coded message
   b. Listening to one end of a telephone conversation
   c. Discovering the richness of the early church
   d. Catching a glimpse of the first century

2. Which New Testament figure(s) planted or led the church in Colossae?
   a. Aquila and Priscilla
   b. Barnabas
   c. Epaphras
   d. Timothy

3. What is the problem that Paul is addressing in Colossae?
   a. Judaizer influence
   b. Jew and gentile relations
   c. Failure to recognize fullness in Christ
   d. Misconceptions about the second coming

4. A believer's identity as God's child is best described as positional truth because the full reality of this relationship is not yet manifested.
   a. True
   b. False

5. A Christian will enjoy his union with Christ in direct proportion to which of the following?
   a. Faith
   b. Knowledge of Scripture
   c. Knowledge of Jesus
   d. Personal holiness

6. The most prominent people in the church are not necessarily the most important people in the church.
   a. True
   b. False

Answer Key—Hidden in Christ

REFLECTION & DISCUSSION QUESTIONS

Before the Video

What Do You Think?

These are personal questions. The answers should be based on your own knowledge and experience.

Scripture Reading

- According to this passage, how can someone who is united to Christ strengthen that union? What dangers are mentioned?

  Paul urges those in Colossae who have received the Lord Jesus Christ to walk in Him, to be rooted in Him, to be established in the faith that they were originally taught, and to abound in thanksgiving to God. In this way, they will be equipped to withstand the dangers Paul mentions: sophisticated philosophy and deceptive arguments that originate from human tradition and have an affinity with the basic principles of the fallen world order.

During the Video

A New Identity

- How did false teaching likely begin and spread in the Colossian church?

  The false teaching in Colossae may have begun with the idea that in order to deal with disappointment in the Christian life, something else was needed. According to this mind-set, trusting in Jesus is fine, but true spiritual fulfillment comes by following certain additional principles and laws. In order to promote an alleged path to spiritual fullness, these false teachers then began to present spiritual practices involving diet, nature, and rhythms of life that they claimed would help Christians find true fulfillment.

- How did Paul respond to the false teaching in Colossae? How did he diagnose the Colossians' actual spiritual problem?

  Paul urged the Colossians not to be deceived by the false teachers' claims because the fullness of Christ was already theirs. There is nothing to be added to Christ. Their real spiritual need, according to Paul, is not to fill up what is lacking in Christ but rather to know the fullness that they have already received but have not fully grasped.

- What benefits are implied by Paul's summary of union with Christ in Colossians 3:1–4?

In Paul's summary of union with Jesus in Colossians 3:1–4, he points out to the Colossian believers that they are united to Jesus in His death, burial, resurrection, ascension to heaven, session at the Father's right hand, and current reign. Paul points out that when Jesus returns to consummate His kingdom, they will also appear with Him in glory.

A New Mentality and a New Destiny

- What question is Dr. Ferguson known to ask candidates during job interviews? What does the answer to this question reveal about a person?

  When he interviews potential church staff members, Dr. Ferguson is known to ask, "What do you think about when you've got nothing else to think about?" A person's answer to this question is an index of his affections. When someone's mind is totally free, it tends to drift toward the things that he values most.

- How does Dr. Ferguson say that Christians will appear at Christ's return?

  Dr. Ferguson observed that at Christ's return, all that God has done by His Spirit in the lives of His people to transform them into the likeness of Christ will be made evident. What is on the inside right now will then appear on the outside. When we meet people in the next life who have lived modest, quiet lives, we will finally behold them for who they truly are.

After the Video

- How did the Colossian false teachers' view of the fullness of Christ compare with Paul's description of the fullness of Christ?

  The false teachers in Colossae were teaching that in order to experience the true fullness of the Christian life, Christians must adopt additional habits and practices. In contrast to this false teaching that sought to add to the gospel, Paul reminded the believers that the fullness of the gospel was already theirs through union with Jesus Christ.

- Why would Jesus consider Himself incomplete without His people?

  The idea that the exalted Christ is incomplete without His people was taught by the early church fathers and echoed centuries later by the Reformers. Because Christ has become the second Adam, because He has united us to Himself, He now considers Himself incomplete without us.

- What story played a part in Dr. Ferguson's conversion to Jesus Christ? How does the person in that story illustrate the significance of union with Christ?

  Dr. Ferguson recounts a story that he heard around the time of his conversion about a businessman who had been moved to an office in Dr. Ferguson's home city. As the businessman was touring the different departments, he noticed the sound of a particular typewriter that could always be heard operating with the same consistency. When he asked about that particular typist, he was told, "Well, that's so-and-so, and she's a Christian." That particular typist demonstrated a faithful consistency in her work as a result of her union with Jesus Christ. The witness to the person of Jesus Christ manifested in her work ethic helped lead to the conversion not just of that businessman but of Dr. Ferguson as well.

REVIEW QUIZ

Lesson 9

1. **B.**
   Dr. Ferguson compares reading certain portions of New Testament letters to listening to one end of a telephone conversation. Half the conversation is fairly well known, but one has to fill in certain gaps in one's understanding in order to fully appreciate or comprehend the conversation as a whole.

2. **C.**
   Paul composed his letter to the Colossians at the request of Epaphras, who either had planted the Colossian church or was one of its pastors at the time.

3. **C.**
   Paul addresses many problems in his letters to the churches of the first century. The problem of the Judaizers is central in Galatians, Jew and gentile relations is a theme in Romans, and questions about the second coming are cleared up in 1 and 2 Thessalonians. The problem in Colossae, as in Galatia, did involve a pernicious influence of false teachers, but it was a different sort from the Judaizers', though both fundamentally denied the fullness that Christians already have in Christ.

4. **B.**
   The label of "positional truth," often used to describe the believer's new status in Christ, puts an unnecessary qualification on the reality of union with Jesus. A believer's new identity in Christ is not merely positional truth; it is the *truth. This is not just a position that a Christian holds; it is the deepest reality of the Christian life.*

5. **C.**
   A Christian's union with Christ is stable and secure because it depends not on the Christian's performance but on Jesus Christ. The extent to which a believer enjoys his union with Christ, however, varies in direct proportion to his knowledge of Jesus Christ. With greater intimacy comes greater joy.

6. **A.**
   Jesus taught that in His kingdom many who are first will be last, and many who are last will be first. In the same way, the people who occupy positions of leadership and prominence in the church are by no means guaranteed to be the greatest in the kingdom of heaven. When we meet one another in glory, we will likely be surprised to behold the true spiritual stature of many who appeared to be lowly and insignificant in this life.

10

Putting Off Sin, Putting On Christ

INTRODUCTION

Paul is equally bold in proclaiming the fullness of the gospel that already belongs to those who are in Christ and in calling on those who are in Christ to pursue holiness relentlessly. For Paul, the glorious grace of God is not a license to abandon Christ's commands but is rather the foundation for a rigorous and disciplined life. In this lesson, Dr. Ferguson will examine Paul's dual exhortations for Christians to put off sin and put on Christ.

LEARNING GOALS

When you have finished this lesson, you should be able to:

- Understand why and how Christians are to put sin to death
- Understand why and how Christians are to put on Christ

KEY IDEAS

- Sanctification is the process of putting sin to death in order to be adorned with the graces of the Lord Jesus Christ.
- Christians can break sin's stranglehold through confession and repentance.
- Christians can put on Christ by setting their affections on Him, pursuing the fruit of the Spirit, and living with confidence in the reality that they are united to Jesus Christ.

REFLECTION & DISCUSSION QUESTIONS

Before the Video

What Do You Think?

Take a moment to answer the following questions. They will prepare you for the lecture.

- What area of sin in your life do you most want to change? Why?

- What strategies for putting sin to death have you found most helpful in your life?

Scripture Reading

The night is far gone; the day is at hand. So then let us cast off the works of darkness and put on the armor of light. Let us walk properly as in the daytime, not in orgies and drunkenness, not in sexual immorality and sensuality, not in quarreling and jealousy. But put on the Lord Jesus Christ, and make no provision for the flesh, to gratify its desires.

—Romans 13:12–14

- What metaphor does Paul use for the two different spiritual worlds that people can inhabit? What does he call Christians to do in light of who they are?

During the Video

Answer the following questions while you watch the video. They will guide you through the lecture.

Putting Off the Old Ways of Sin *0:00–20:20*

- What claim did the nineteenth-century Scotsman Thomas Chalmers make about the process of mortifying sin?

- Which three categories of sin does Paul list and expound on in Colossians 3:5–11?

- What point does Dr. Ferguson make about the similarities and differences in the body of Christ?

Putting On the New Ways of Christ *20:20–23:32*

- How did Augustine personally encounter Paul's exhortation to put on Jesus Christ?
- What aspect of the ministry of Bishop Ambrose of Milan made the greatest impact on Augustine? Why is this surprising?

After the Video

Answer the following questions after you have finished the lecture. They will help you identify and summarize the major points.

- Why does Satan tend to aim his arrows of spiritual warfare at the area of human sexuality?

  If you are in a group, have the members identify additional areas of life where Satan's spiritual attacks are common.
- What thought does Dr. Ferguson suggest thinking when we encounter people at church with whom we would rather not associate?

  If you are in a group, have the members answer the following question: How might this thought transform your relationship with a specific person you are inclined to avoid?
- Why does Paul appear to break his own rule about not mentioning certain sins by listing so many damaging sins in Colossians 3:5–9?

  If you are in a group, have the members interact with the following statement: We are delivered from these things only when we admit what they really are. Do you agree or disagree? Explain.

PRAYER

Commit what you have learned from God's Word in this lesson to prayer.

- Praise God for the freedom in Christ from sin's bondage.
- Confess a specific area of sin in your life that you need to put off.
- Thank God for leading you to repentance and new life in Christ.
- Ask God to help you put on Christ in an area of your life where you struggle to live for Him.

REVIEW QUIZ

Use these multiple-choice questions to measure what you learned from this lesson.

1. Which of the following theologians argued that Christians cannot put sin to death without replacing it with the fruit of the Spirit?
   a. Ambrose of Milan
   b. Augustine of Hippo
   c. Charles Haddon Spurgeon
   d. Thomas Chalmers
2. Paul addresses all the following categories of sin in Colossians 3:5–11 *except*:
   a. Sexual sins
   b. Sins of omission
   c. Sins of the mouth
   d. Sins that disrupt the fellowship of believers
3. What reality undergirds the rigorous imperatives that Paul presents in Colossians 3?
   a. Christians are called to work out their salvation with fear and trembling.
   b. In whatever they do, Christians are to live as for God and not for people.
   c. As Christ's people, Christians are united to Him.
   d. Friendship with the world is enmity toward God.
4. Which term can summarize the behaviors that Paul tells believers to put on?
   a. "Spirit-led"
   b. "Born again"
   c. "Christlikeness"
   d. "*Tolle lege*"
5. Which statement from Scripture turned Augustine's life around for Christ?
   a. "Be holy, for I am holy."
   b. "For by grace you have been saved through faith."
   c. "Put on the Lord Jesus Christ, and make no provision for the flesh."
   d. "The righteous shall live by faith."
6. Which of the following does Dr. Ferguson describe as the engine that drives change in the life of a believer?
   a. Moral fortitude
   b. Doctrinal orthodoxy
   c. Fear of the consequences of sin
   d. Knowledge of one's union with Christ

Answer Key—
Putting Off Sin, Putting On Christ

REFLECTION & DISCUSSION QUESTIONS

Before the Video

What Do You Think?

These are personal questions. The answers should be based on your own knowledge and experience.

Scripture Reading

- What metaphor does Paul use for the two different spiritual worlds that people can inhabit? What does he call Christians to do in light of who they are?

  These verses describe the old world of union with Adam and the new world of union with Christ in terms of the contrast between the darkness of night and the light of day. Paul declares to the Roman believers that the day has come; therefore, they are to walk in a manner that is appropriate for those who live in the day. Rather than gratify the desires of the flesh, they are to put on the Lord Jesus Christ.

During the Video

Putting Off the Old Ways of Sin

- What claim did the nineteenth-century Scotsman Thomas Chalmers make about the process of mortifying sin?

  The nineteenth-century Scottish churchman Thomas Chalmers noted in his sermon "The Expulsive Power of a New Affection" that a Christian's efforts to mortify sin will be in vain unless he expels sinful characteristics by replacing them with the fruit of the Holy Spirit. In other words, we cannot get rid of sinful desires unless we replace them with godly desires.

- Which three categories of sin does Paul list and expound on in Colossians 3:5–11?

  In order to describe specific sins that believers are to put off, Paul first lists a variety of private sins involving a person's inner personal life, particularly sexual activities, in verse 5. He proceeds to discuss sins of the mouth that affect human relationships in verse 8. He then concludes by talking about sins that disrupt Christian fellowship in verse 9.

- What point does Dr. Ferguson make about the similarities and differences in the body of Christ?

Dr. Ferguson used a story to illustrate the point that human eyes are naturally drawn to similarities, and it is often only when we look into the similarities that we begin to understand the differences. This principle applies to the body of Christ in the sense that, though His body is vast and diverse, all believers share a common identity in Christ.

Putting On the New Ways of Christ

- How did Augustine personally encounter Paul's exhortation to put on Jesus Christ?

  Augustine's conversion, recorded in his Confessions, *took place when he heard a child's voice in the distance repeating the words* tolle lege, *which mean "take up and read." He picked up a copy of the Bible and read the words of Romans 13:14: "Put on the Lord Jesus Christ, and make no provision for the flesh, to gratify its desires." This statement, which summarizes the main thrust of Paul's teaching in Colossians 3, convicted Augustine of his need to turn from his life of sin and place his trust in Jesus.*

- What aspect of the ministry of Bishop Ambrose of Milan made the greatest impact on Augustine? Why is this surprising?

  In his Confessions, *Augustine wrote that when he was struggling spiritually and arrived in the city of Milan, he went to listen to Ambrose preach. Although Ambrose was known as a great orator, it was actually the bishop's kindness to Augustine that had the greatest effect on him. This is surprising because one would expect that Augustine, the great intellectual and student of oration, would have been most interested in Ambrose's intellect and eloquence. But the reality that Augustine was most influenced by Ambrose's kindness can serve as a reminder that all Christians, regardless of their intellectual abilities, can minister to the lost by demonstrating a Christlike spirit.*

After the Video

- Why does Satan tend to aim his arrows of spiritual warfare at the area of human sexuality?

  The worst things tend to be corruptions of the best things. One of God's greatest gifts to humanity is the reality that He has made us in the image of God, male and female, for family life. For this reason, the devil has always sought to make inroads into this sacred area of life by destroying our personal purity and relationships with those who are closest to us. By wreaking havoc in the family, Satan can rob us of some of God's most precious blessings and use them to inflict pain in place of the joy that God intended.

- What thought does Dr. Ferguson suggest thinking when we encounter people at church with whom we would rather not associate?

  Dr. Ferguson pointed out that most churches include people whom others tend to avoid. He challenges us to think of the person in our church from whom we naturally turn away whenever we see the person. What would happen if your first thought toward that person was "Here is someone that the Lord of glory is unashamed to indwell"?

- Why does Paul appear to break his own rule about not mentioning certain sins by listing so many damaging sins in Colossians 3:5–9?

  Paul's catalogue of severe sins in Colossians 3 is intended to encourage the practice of confession and repentance. By citing examples of particularly damaging sins, he is bringing these acts out of darkness and privacy and into the open so that believers will admit their sin for what it really is. Underlying Paul's approach is the reality that we are delivered from these enslaving sins only when we admit what they really are in the presence of God. This act of open confession can begin to break the stranglehold that such sins can have on us.

REVIEW QUIZ

Lesson 10

1. **D.**
   The nineteenth-century Scottish churchman Thomas Chalmers observed in his sermon "The Expulsive Power of a New Affection" that Christians will fail in their efforts to mortify sin unless they intentionally replace their sins with the fruit of the Spirit.

2. **B.**
   Writing to the Colossian believers in Colossians 3:5–11, Paul describes three categories of sin in vivid detail. These three categories include sexual sins in a believer's private life, sins of the mouth that influence a believer's relationships with others, and sins in community that disrupt the fellowship of the body of believers.

3. **C.**
   In contrast to the idea that the gospel of grace rules out imperatives in the Christian life, Paul presents rigorous commands for believers to follow. The truth that undergirds these imperatives is the reality that as Christ's people we are united to Him. As a result, we are to put behind us the old worldly order to establish an order that is faithful to our Lord Jesus Christ.

4. **C.**
   All the behaviors that Paul urges believers to put on can be summarized under the heading "Christlikeness." In short, it is the very character of Jesus that believers appropriate for themselves once they are united to Christ.

5. **C.**
   Augustine records in his Confessions *how he was converted to Christ as a result of picking up a New Testament and reading, "Put on the Lord Jesus Christ, and make no provision for the flesh, to gratify its desires." These words from Romans 13:14*

summarize the message of Colossians 3:5–17 and spoke powerfully to Augustine as someone who had spent years attempting to gratify his sinful desires.

6. **D.**

   Dr. Ferguson concluded this lecture by identifying knowledge of union with Christ as the engine that drives change in a believer's life. This statement reflects the reality that Christians already possess all the fullness of the Christian life in Jesus. By believing this and living into this reality, they can truly begin to revel in this fullness.

11

The Vine & the Branches

INTRODUCTION

The life and writings of the Apostle Paul are saturated with the theme of union with Jesus Christ. Yet this notion of being united to Christ did not originate with Paul. Jesus Himself spoke with His disciples about the vital importance of being united to Him. In this lesson, we will explore Christ's teaching on the vine and the branches in John 15 and learn, from Jesus' own words, why our union with Him is the most important part of our lives.

LEARNING GOALS

When you have finished this lesson, you should be able to:

- Summarize Jesus' teaching of the vine and the branches in John 15:1–11
- Describe four principles of union with Christ that Jesus articulates in John 15

KEY IDEAS

- Our union with Christ is the source of all fruitfulness in our lives.
- Our union with Christ involves pruning if we are to bear fruit.
- Our union with Christ is nurtured and nourished by the Word of God.
- The most apparent fruit of our union with Christ is love.

REFLECTION & DISCUSSION QUESTIONS

Before the Video

What Do You Think?

Take a moment to answer the following questions. They will prepare you for the lecture.

- How should Christians understand the trials and difficulties they experience in life? Are hard times evidence of God's absence, love, punishment, or something else?

- Should church be a place full of sinful people or holy people? Explain your answer.

- What makes the love of Jesus different from other kinds of love?

Scripture Reading

"This is my commandment, that you love one another as I have loved you. Greater love has no one than this, that someone lay down his life for his friends. You are my friends if you do what I command you. No longer do I call you servants, for the servant does not know what his master is doing; but I have called you friends, for all that I have heard from my Father I have made known to you. You did not choose me, but I chose you and appointed you that you should go and bear fruit and that your fruit should abide, so that whatever you ask the Father in my name, he may give it to you. These things I command you, so that you will love one another."

—John 15:12–17

- How does Jesus describe His love for His people in these verses? How does He desire that this love be manifested in their lives?

During the Video

Answer the following questions while you watch the video. They will guide you through the lecture.

Fruitful and Pruned Branches *0:00–13:52*

- In light of the fact that union with Christ is the source of our fruitfulness, what should Christians focus on? What should Christians not focus on?

- For what two reasons does a vinedresser prune the vines?

Nourished by the Word, Fruitful in Love *13:52–23:21*

- How does our culture's "can do" attitude influence our approach to the Christian life? How does this approach differ from the teaching of the New Testament?

- How does Christian love differ from the notion of love that is culturally prominent?

After the Video

Answer the following questions after you have finished the lecture. They will help you identify and summarize the major points.

- How did Jesus seek to comfort His disciples as He was about to leave them? How do believers today benefit from the things Jesus spoke of?

  If you are in a group, have the members read John 16:5–15. What blessings did Jesus promise to His disciples through the Holy Spirit? What blessings does the Spirit impart to believers today?

- "There is not a random stroke in it all, nothing cut away which it would not have been a loss to keep and gain to lose." What is the meaning behind this statement?

  If you are in a group, have the members discuss ways that God works through painful circumstances to make His people more fruitful.

- According to Dr. Ferguson, why do some people hear exactly what they need to hear in a sermon?

  If you are in a group, have the members describe a time when Christ spoke powerfully to them through the preaching of His Word.

PRAYER

Commit what you have learned from God's Word in this lesson to prayer.

- Praise God for nourishing your growth in grace through union with His Son.
- Confess ways that you have sought nourishment apart from Christ and His Word.
- Thank God for sending His Spirit to dwell in you and unite you to Christ.
- Ask God to help you endure your pruning, that you might bear greater fruit for Him.

REVIEW QUIZ

Use these multiple-choice questions to measure what you learned from this lesson.

1. Which of the following is *not* a principle of union with Christ found in Jesus' teaching on the vine and the branches?
   a. This union bears love as its most obvious fruit.
   b. This union is nurtured and nourished by a believer's good works.
   c. This union is the source of all fruitfulness in a believer's life.
   d. This union requires pruning in the life of a believer.

2. How did one of Dr. Ferguson's previous ministers describe the Christian life?
   a. Christians learn to live mechanically.
   b. Christians learn to do the natural thing supernaturally.
   c. Christians learn to do the supernatural thing naturally.
   d. Christians learn to reject the natural and embrace the supernatural.

3. According to Dr. Ferguson, which of the following is true about the Christian who is never pruned?
   a. The Christian who is never pruned becomes vulnerable to spiritual pride.
   b. The Christian who is never pruned enjoys God's special favor.
   c. The Christian who is never pruned is a Christian in name only.
   d. The Christian who is never pruned will never grow.

4. How does a Christian grow strong in his union with Christ?
   a. By denying sinful desires and embracing a holy lifestyle
   b. By experiencing powerful moments in worship
   c. By feeding on God's Word
   d. By loving others

5. Which metaphor best describes the ministry of the Word that takes place in a local church?
   a. Classroom
   b. Marketplace
   c. Showroom
   d. Workshop

6. What does union with Christ ultimately create in a believer?
   a. A new view of the world
   b. A likeness to Jesus Christ
   c. A thorough moral transformation
   d. A more complete understanding of God's Word

Answer Key—The Vine & the Branches

REFLECTION & DISCUSSION QUESTIONS

Before the Video

What Do You Think?

These are personal questions. The answers should be based on your own knowledge and experience.

Scripture Reading

- How does Jesus describe His love for His people in these verses? How does He desire that this love be manifested in their lives?

  On the heels of His discussion of the vine and the branches in John 15:1–11, Jesus commands His followers to love one another as He has loved them. Jesus' love for His people is described in terms of His acts of choosing them, voluntarily laying down His life for them, making known to them what He has received from the Father, and promising that they will receive what they ask for in His name. Implied in His command is that they are to be united to one another as they are united to Him and that they are to lay down their lives for one another in imitation of Christ's life.

During the Video

Fruitful and Pruned Branches

- In light of the fact that union with Christ is the source of our fruitfulness, what should Christians focus on? What should Christians not focus on?

  In response to the reality of union with Christ, Christians are not to fixate on the question of how to bear fruit and thereby bring about this fruitfulness by themselves. Rather, they are to continue living in union and communion with the Lord Jesus Christ. As they abide in Him, He will bring about a rich harvest of fruit in their lives.

- For what two reasons does a vinedresser prune the vines?

  There are two reasons why a vinedresser prunes the vines in his care: (1) to cut away the portions of the vines that will not bear fruit, and (2) to prune the vines in order to promote the growth of richer, better, and more abundant fruit. In the same way, Christ prunes His people in order to remove the parts of us that do not bear fruit and increase our fruitfulness beyond what it would be if we were left unpruned.

Nourished by the Word, Fruitful in Love

- How does our culture's "can do" attitude influence our approach to the Christian life? How does this approach differ from the teaching of the New Testament?

  The United States is characterized by a "can do" culture, which translates into a pragmatic, action-driven approach to the Christian life. Christians with this mind-set, therefore, simply want to be told what to do, and they will find a way to do it. In contrast, the New Testament teaches that the Word of God does the work itself. Therefore, "can do" Christians are challenged simply to bring themselves into the Lord's presence and allow Him, through His Word and by His Spirit, to bring about change in their lives.

- How does Christian love differ from the notion of love that is culturally prominent?

  The sentiment of the Beatles' song "All You Need Is Love" is emblematic of the notion of love that is common in our culture, in which love is a generic feeling of warmth and goodwill. In contrast to this perception of love, Jesus calls His followers to live out a radical commitment to one another's well-being. It is through believers' demonstration of love to one another that the world will know that we are united to Christ.

After the Video

- How did Jesus seek to comfort His disciples as He was about to leave them? How do believers today benefit from the things Jesus spoke of?

  To alleviate His disciples' concern over His coming departure, Jesus told them that the Spirit would come to them. The same Spirit who had been Jesus' companion, in whose power Jesus had done mighty works, in whom Jesus would offer Himself to the Father, who would energize Jesus' resurrection—this Spirit would descend on Christ's people on the day of Pentecost. Through His indwelling, the Spirit would bring Jesus even nearer to the disciples than He had been when He lived among them. Because the Spirit dwells within us, believers today are united to Jesus and to one another.

- "There is not a random stroke in it all, nothing cut away which it would not have been a loss to keep and gain to lose." What is the meaning behind this statement?

  Amy Carmichael, an influential Protestant missionary to India in the late nineteenth and early twentieth centuries, observed that God's pruning of the believer, while painful at the time, is in a Christian's long-term best interests because he is being conformed to the image of Jesus Christ.

- According to Dr. Ferguson, why do some people hear exactly what they need to hear in a sermon?

  Dr. Ferguson described a phenomenon, familiar to preachers, in which they may sense that the words they say are not what congregants need to hear; yet God works powerfully to impress on the hearts of the listeners exactly what they do need to hear. This occurs because when Christ's Word is preached, Christ Himself is preaching it. What listeners experience as they hear God's Word being proclaimed is the presence of Christ Himself. As the Word dwells in us richly, Christ dwells within us, and we dwell within Him. This reality of how Christ inhabits the ministry of the Word offers great encouragement to preachers and church members alike.

REVIEW QUIZ

Lesson 11

1. **B.**
   Four basic principles of union with Christ found in Jesus' teaching on the vine and the branches are that this union (1) is the source of all fruitfulness in a believer's life, (2) requires pruning in the life of a believer, (3) is nurtured and nourished by God's Word—not a person's good works—and (4) bears love as its most obvious fruit.

2. **C.**
   William Still, who had served as Dr. Ferguson's minister during his days as a student, observed that what characterizes the Christian is that he learns to do the supernatural naturally. This is another way of saying that the Christian life is not mechanical but that the supernatural occurs in a believer's life in a natural, organic way. As we abide in Christ, the effects of His new creation gradually reshape who we are and how we live.

3. **D.**
   Dr. Ferguson states in no uncertain terms that the Christian who is never pruned will never grow. Just as a vine will reach its highest level of fruitfulness only through constant pruning, it is only through God's work of pruning us that we bear the most abundant fruit for Christ.

4. **C.**
   Though a variety of important fruit will emerge out of a believer's union with Christ, holy living and love for others are not what strengthen a person's union with the Lord. Rather, the key to growing strong in union with Christ is to be fed on His Word.

5. **D.**
   Dr. Ferguson recalls seeing a church sign that read, "Workshop inside, showroom upstairs." This playful description illustrates the reality that the church is not a showroom where perfect people are on display. Rather, it is a workshop where God is crafting imperfect sinners into the image of Christ through the ministry of His Word.

6. **B.**
   The ultimate fruit of union with Jesus Christ is that God creates in His people a likeness to the Christ to whom believers are united.

12

Sharing in His Death & Resurrection

INTRODUCTION

Our union with Christ is not only the centerpiece our spiritual lives. It also encompasses the entirety of our spiritual lives. In this final lesson, Dr. Ferguson explores a vital but neglected dimension of a believer's union with Christ, a union with His suffering. Just as being united to the death and resurrection of Christ internally brings about a changed spiritual mind-set, so also being united to His death and resurrection externally brings about both suffering and fruitfulness that cannot be achieved any other way.

LEARNING GOALS

When you have finished this lesson, you should be able to:

- Describe the importance of union with Christ for God's people throughout history
- Differentiate between the internal and external effects of being united to Jesus
- Explain the link between union with Christ's suffering and union with His fruitfulness

KEY IDEAS

- A Christian's union with Christ is experienced both inwardly through spiritual transformation and outwardly through the rhythm of death and resurrection.
- As Christians carry about in their mortal bodies the death of Jesus Christ, the life of Jesus Christ is also manifested in them.
- A Christian's union with Jesus Christ can find completion only in the fruitfulness that comes by sharing in His suffering.

REFLECTION & DISCUSSION QUESTIONS

Before the Video

What Do You Think?

Take a moment to answer the following questions. They will prepare you for the lecture.

- How has your relationship with Christ changed or deepened as a result of this study on union with Him?

- What have you learned from this teaching series that you are most excited to share with others?

Scripture Reading

Now I rejoice in my sufferings for your sake, and in my flesh I am filling up what is lacking in Christ's afflictions for the sake of his body, that is, the church, of which I became a minister according to the stewardship from God that was given to me for you, to make the word of God fully known, the mystery hidden for ages and generations but now revealed to his saints. To them God chose to make known how great among the Gentiles are the riches of the glory of this mystery, which is Christ in you, the hope of glory. Him we proclaim, warning everyone and teaching everyone with all wisdom, that we may present everyone mature in Christ. For this I toil, struggling with all his energy that he powerfully works within me.

—Colossians 1:24–29

- What goals drive Paul's ministry? What is the mystery that has now been made known?

During the Video

Answer the following questions while you watch the video. They will guide you through the lecture.

The Double Union Displayed in Scripture *0:00–8:46*

- What is the meaning of a double mortification and vivification in the lives of believers?

- How did God's people experience union with Christ in the Old Testament?

Sharing in His Suffering and Fruitfulness *8:46–23:13*

- What point does Paul make about his experience of union with Christ in Colossians 1:24?

- What does Paul mean when he mentions in 2 Corinthians 13:4 that Christians are weak in Christ?

- According to 2 Corinthians 1:4–5, what did Paul taste in his affliction that he did not taste in his comfort?

After the Video

Answer the following questions after you have finished the lecture. They will help you identify and summarize the major points.

- What are some of the points that Dr. Ferguson mentioned in his review of this teaching series at the beginning of this lesson?

  If you are in a group, have the members discuss some of the truths they have encountered in this teaching series that they have found most helpful in their understanding of their own union with Christ.

- How does Joseph's life serve as a reverse echo of the life of Jesus?

  If you are in a group, have the members discuss the following question: How have you seen echoes of Jesus in the lives of Christians that you have known?

- What is the pattern for bearing fruit that God used in Jesus' life and is now using in our lives?

  If you are in a group, have the members consider practical ways in which they can encourage others to both grow in fruitfulness and provide feedback about fruitfulness observed in their own lives.

PRAYER

Commit what you have learned from God's Word in this lesson to prayer.

- Praise God for His sovereign work of uniting repentant sinners to Christ by faith throughout history.

- Confess your personal fears or reluctance when it comes to sharing in Christ's suffering.
- Thank God for using hardships in your life to produce fruitfulness, blessing, and comfort.
- Ask God to help you continue to grow in your union with Jesus and your resemblance to Him.

REVIEW QUIZ

Use these multiple-choice questions to measure what you learned from this lesson.

1. Which of the following theologians articulated the dual reality of *mortificatio duplex* and *vivificatio duplex* in the Christian life?
   a. Thomas Chalmers
   b. John Calvin
   c. Robert Murray M'Cheyne
   d. Charles Haddon Spurgeon
2. Where did Paul's understanding of union with Christ emerge from?
   a. Discovering the doctrine of justification by faith alone
   b. Experiencing suffering for the sake of Jesus Christ
   c. Realizing that persecuting Christians was the same as persecuting Christ
   d. Trusting Jesus Christ as his personal Savior and Lord
3. For whose sake does Paul see himself as suffering in Colossians 1:24?
   a. For his own sake
   b. For the sake of Jesus Christ
   c. For the sake of other Christians
   d. For the sake of those who will come to faith through his sufferings
4. According to Dr. Ferguson, what kind of rhythm leads to fruitfulness in a Christian's life?
   a. A rhythm of death and resurrection
   b. A rhythm of personal evangelism
   c. A rhythm of sacrifice in Jesus' name
   d. A rhythm of spiritual discipline
5. In whose life did Paul encounter the idea of showing the life of Christ by carrying around the death of Christ?
   a. Luke
   b. Joseph
   c. Peter
   d. Stephen

6. What practical benefit did Paul's afflictions bring to his ministry?
   a. A greater drive to share the gospel
   b. Compassion and sympathy from others
   c. Powerful sermon illustrations
   d. The capacity to comfort others who suffer

Answer Key—Sharing in His Death & Resurrection

REFLECTION & DISCUSSION QUESTIONS

Before the Video

What Do You Think?

These are personal questions. The answers should be based on your own knowledge and experience.

Scripture Reading

- What goals drive Paul's ministry? What is the mystery that has now been made known?

  Colossians 1:24–29 offers a glimpse into the passions and desires that drive Paul's labor for the Lord. For the sake of Christ's body, he gladly endures suffering and hardship. He desires to make God's Word and the mystery of the gospel known. He concludes by saying that this proclamation and toil is also driven by his intention of presenting the believers to Christ as mature disciples. At the centerpiece of Paul's life and ministry is the proclamation of the mystery of the gospel that God is making known among the gentiles the mystery of Christ in His people, the hope of glory.

During the Video

The Double Union Displayed in Scripture

- What is the meaning of a double mortification and vivification in the lives of believers?

  A believer's union with Christ in His death and resurrection is worked out both inwardly and outwardly in the Christian life. John Calvin emphasized this concept in his vocabulary of double mortification, which he called a mortificatio duplex, *and double vivification, which he described as* vivificatio duplex. *Therefore, just as union with Christ's death and resurrection results in the inner experience of putting off sin and putting on Christ, it also results in the outer experience of sharing in His suffering and in His fruitfulness.*

- How did God's people experience union with Christ in the Old Testament?

  Even before Jesus came to earth and died on the cross, God's people still experienced union with Him through their faith that God would keep His covenant promises to them. Old Testament saints were therefore united in that promise to the Christ who would later die and rise. Consequently, as we survey the Old Testament, we can see that they too put away sin and, with the help of the Spirit, put on graces that we recognize as Christlike graces.

Sharing in His Suffering and Fruitfulness

- What point does Paul make about his experience of union with Christ in Colossians 1:24?

  Speaking of his own experience of being united to Christ, Paul states that for the sake of the church he is filling up what is lacking in the sufferings of Christ. Paul is not claiming that anything is lacking in Jesus' suffering. Rather, he is pointing out that the full outworking of his own union with Christ has not come to its completion because he has not yet suffered as Christ suffered. Therefore, it is as he endures suffering that Paul's experience of union with Christ is becoming more complete, sharing in the sufferings of Christ so that in Christ he may be fruitful in the church.

- What does Paul mean when he mentions in 2 Corinthians 13:4 that Christians are weak in Christ?

  When Paul remarks that "we also are weak in him" in 2 Corinthians 13:4, he expresses a truth that seems out of step with the victorious nature of the gospel that he articulates elsewhere. In essence, Paul is saying that the weakness he has experienced was the fruit of his union with a Christ who was weakened in crucifixion. Therefore, those who are in Christ can expect to experience great weakness because it is out of great weakness in Christ that believers also experience great fruitfulness in Christ.

- According to 2 Corinthians 1:4–5, what did Paul taste in his affliction that he did not taste in his comfort?

  In the opening verses of 2 Corinthians, Paul expresses his praise to God, who has comforted him in all his afflictions so that he may comfort others. These verses reveal that in his sufferings, Paul has gained the capacity to minister to others in a way that he would not be able to do if he had not experienced episodes of suffering in his own life. Having shared abundantly in Christ's sufferings, Paul is now able to share Christ's comfort abundantly with others.

After the Video

- What are some of the points that Dr. Ferguson mentioned in his review of this teaching series at the beginning of this lesson?

  Dr. Ferguson reviewed a number of important points from this teaching series: (1) union with Christ is an important theme in the New Testament, especially since Paul uses the expression "in Christ," "in the Lord," or "in Him" more than 160 times; (2) as the church fathers pointed out, Jesus considers Himself incomplete without the saints from every age who are united to Him by faith; (3) Jesus Christ, by His work on the cross, has brought redeemed sinners together into a new family that is spiritually distinct from the old family in Adam, because Christians are now under a new head, Jesus Christ; (4) Jesus taught that, as branches connected to His vine, believers should expect to be pruned, since hardships and trials produce His image and His fruitfulness within them.

- How does Joseph's life serve as a reverse echo of the life of Jesus?

  Joseph serves as a helpful illustration of the effects of union with Christ. United to Christ by his faith in God's promise, Joseph shares in the suffering, humiliation, and death of Christ. Joseph's life is like a reverse echo of Jesus' life. Like Jesus, Joseph is falsely accused and despised. Additionally, in the providence of God, Joseph is then exalted, raised up to a new kind of life, and brings what Genesis calls "salvation," physical salvation to the whole Mediterranean area. In this way, he shares externally in the dying and rising of the Lord Jesus Christ.

- What is the pattern for bearing fruit that God used in Jesus' life and is now using in our lives?

  As we experience suffering and hardship in our lives, we can take heart that God is working within us. After all, it was through the pattern of suffering and dying that Jesus bore fruit. As He transforms us into His likeness to bear fruit, He uses the same pattern on us. In truth, there is no other way. God has a better pattern because this is the pattern that works. When we begin to view the whole of our Christian lives through this lens, we will see this pattern working itself out and can rejoice amid our afflictions that God is bringing about holy fruit in our lives.

REVIEW QUIZ

Lesson 12

1. **B.**
   Calvin emphasized the concept of double mortification, which he called a mortificatio duplex, *and double vivification, which he described as* vivificatio duplex. *Therefore, just as union with Christ's death and resurrection results in the inner experience of putting off sin and putting on Christ, it also results in the outer experience of sharing in His suffering and in His fruitfulness.*

2. **C.**
   Paul's experience on the Damascus road, in which Jesus asked Paul why he was persecuting Him, opened Paul's eyes to the reality that persecuting Christians was the same as persecuting Jesus. This is where Paul's understanding of union with Christ, and his understanding of his own life and ministry, emerged.

3. **C.**
   Paul notes in Colossians 1:24 that his suffering is for the sake of Jesus' church. As the fullness of Christ's suffering is added to him, the result will be an increased fruitfulness for the gospel that will benefit other believers and the church as a whole.

4. **A.**
   Although practices such as spiritual disciplines, personal evangelism, and self-denial are important parts of the Christian life, it is the rhythm of death and resurrection that believers experience in union with Jesus that produces long-term fruitfulness in their lives, just as it did in the life of Jesus Himself.

5. **D.**
   In observing the martyrdom of Stephen, who carried in his body union and communion with the crucified Savior, the young Saul of Tarsus encountered the reality of union with Christ in a powerful way that continued to capture his imagination and fuel his theological growth years into his ministry as an Apostle.

6. **D.**
   Writing in 2 Corinthians 2:4, Paul celebrates the fact that as he experiences God's comfort in the midst of his afflictions, he is better able to comfort others with the comfort that he himself has received.